Blessed

FIRST RECONCILIATION

My name is

GHadd ley

I am blessed, and God made me wonderfully
and marvelously in his own image.
Jesus wants me to become
the-best-version-of-myself,
grow in virtue, and live a holy life.

On this date

Jesus is going to forgive all of my sins
during my First Reconciliation.
I am truly blessed.

In accord with the *Code of Canon Law*,
I hereby grant the *Imprimatur* ("Permission to Publish") for *Blessed*.

Most Reverend Dennis M. Schnurr
Archbishop of Cincinnati
Archdiocese of Cincinnati
Cincinnati, Ohio
December 15, 2016

The *Imprimatur* ("Permission to Publish") is a declaration that a book is considered to be free of doctrinal or moral error. It is not implied that those who have granted the *Imprimatur* agree with the contents, opinions, or statements expressed.

Table of Contents

Session 6: It's Only the Beginning   177

My Little Catechism   203

Acknowledgments   238

1
You Are Blessed!

God, our loving Father,
thank you for all the ways you bless me.
Help me to be aware that every person,
place, and adventure I experience is an
opportunity to love you more.
Fill me with a desire to change and to grow,
and give me the grace to become
the-best-version-of-myself in
every moment of every day.

Amen.

Welcome

Welcome. We are beginning a great journey!

You are a child of God. You are part of the largest and most famous family in the world: the Catholic Church. You are blessed.

God wants you to always feel welcome in his presence, in his Church, and as a member of his family.

You are the son or daughter of a great King.

You may think of yourself as a boy or a girl, as young or old, as black or white, as American or Chinese, but first and foremost, you are a child of God. He is the great King, and you are his son or daughter. We all have this in common. God is our Father.

You Are Blessed

You are blessed. What does it mean to be blessed? It means that God loves you and showers you with gifts.

You are blessed in so many ways, but every blessing you experience flows from the first blessing. You are a child of God. This is the original blessing.

What's the best gift you have ever received?

You may think it is a bike, a baseball bat, a dress, a bracelet, or a video game. But this is not true.

The best gift you have ever received is LIFE. Life makes every other gift possible. Without life, you wouldn't be able to enjoy any other gift!

This is just one of a thousand reasons why life is sacred. God loves life.

The very first thing we read about in the Bible is how God created everything. Then God looked at all he had created and said, "It is good" (Genesis 1:31).

You are blessed in so many ways, but every blessing flows from the blessing of life.

You may be blessed to run like the wind, but if God had not given you life, you wouldn't be able to do that. You may be blessed to eat ice cream, but only because God gave you the original blessing.

You may be blessed to sing like an angel, but only because God gave you life first.

God has given you life and made you his child. You are blessed.

Count Your Blessings

There is an ancient Jewish saying, "Count your blessings!" Jewish rabbis encourage their people to count their blessings each day and see if they can get to one hundred.

Counting our blessings leads us to gratitude. When we count our blessings, we become full of joy and gratitude. God loves a grateful heart. As children of God we should try to begin and end each day with gratitude.

God blesses us in lots of ways. When we count our blessings we are really saying THANK YOU to God for all the fabulous talents, things, people, experiences, and opportunities he gives us.

When someone asks, "How are you?" rather than just saying "good" or "fine," you can say, "I am blessed!" It helps us to remember this, and it reminds others that they are blessed, too.

What are some of the ways God has blessed you?

My Gratitude List

I am grateful for . . .

oufanl's

Food

water

dog's

corrs

air

cufe bed

familyd's

home

freinds

Art

Sicins

My Journey with God

We are all children of God. This makes us all much more alike than we are different. Too often we focus on our differences rather than remembering that we are all brothers and sisters, that we are all children of the same great King.

God gave you life, and he has designed a great journey just for you. Along the way there are going to be some very important moments in your journey.

Baptism

First, there was your Baptism, which was the beginning of your new life in Jesus. This is when you became a member of his Church and joined the largest and most famous family in the world, the Catholic Church.

When and where were you baptized?

First Reconciliation

Now, you are preparing for your First Reconciliation. We all mess up from time to time. We all do things that offend God and place obstacles between him and us. When we get separated from God we become unhappy. Reconciliation removes these obstacles and fills our hearts and souls with joy again.

When will you receive the blessing of your First Reconciliation? I will receive my First Reconciliation on...

First Communion

Before too long, the blessing of Reconciliation will prepare you for your First Communion. Receiving Jesus in the Eucharist is one of the greatest blessings of our lives.

When will you receive Jesus in the Eucharist for the first time? I will receive my First Communion on...

Confirmation

When you are a little older, you will be blessed again when you receive the Sacrament of Confirmation. Confirmation reminds us that in Baptism, God blessed us with a special mission and filled us with the Holy Spirit. It reminds us of these incredible blessings and gives us the courage and wisdom to live out the mission God has given us.

Marriage

Later in life, God may bless you again with Marriage or Holy Orders. In the Sacrament of Marriage, God brings a man and woman together to cherish each other, to live a holy life together, and to help each other become the-best-version-of-themselves, grow in virtue, and get to heaven.

Holy Orders

God calls some people to become priests, deacons, and bishops through the Sacrament of Holy Orders.

Anointing Of The Sick

If along your journey you get sick and need God's healing for body, mind, or spirit, you will be blessed with the Anointing of the Sick.

You are on a great journey with God. Along the way you will experience these great Catholic Moments, which we call the Seven Sacraments. Each of these Moments is a blessing. They are all connected. These great Moments are designed by God to help you live a good life here on earth, and they prepare you to live with God in heaven forever.

You are blessed.

From the Bible: Gratitude

When we take time to pray, reflect, and count our blessings, we realize that God has blessed us in so many ways. Gratitude is the best response to any blessing. There is a wonderful story in the Gospel of Luke about gratitude.

One day while Jesus was traveling to Jerusalem, ten men with leprosy approached him and asked him to cure them. Most people would not go anywhere near a person with leprosy because the disease is very contagious, but Jesus had mercy on them.

He blessed them and said, "Go and show yourselves to the priests." Along the way, the lepers realized that they had been healed. It was a miracle!

When one of the lepers saw that he was cured of this horrible disease, he was filled with joy and immediately went back to Jesus and praised him at the top of his voice. Jesus asked the man, "Where are the others?"

Adapted from Luke 17:11–19

Jesus had cured all ten lepers, but only one said thank you. Jesus had just changed their lives forever, but they couldn't even be bothered to come back and say thank you. That's rude, don't you think?

Perhaps the others intended to thank Jesus, but they got distracted with life. Maybe they thought to themselves, "I will thank Jesus tomorrow, or next week."

The one leper who came back teaches us many lessons.

1. **Be grateful when God blesses you.**

2. **It's rude not to be grateful.**

3. **When God blesses you abundantly, say thank you in a big way. The leper who did come back didn't just whisper thank you into Jesus' ear. He praised Jesus at the top of his voice.**

4. **Don't put off important things. That includes your daily prayer and going to church. When did the one leper go back and thank Jesus? Immediately. He didn't put it off.**

5. **When we acknowledge God's blessings we become filled with joy.**

Every person in every Bible story has a lesson to teach you. Each Sunday at Mass, think about the people in the readings and what lesson God is trying to teach you through their lives.

I Am Blessed. I Am Grateful.

One of the ways we can love God is by being grateful for all the ways he has blessed us. God blesses us in a thousand ways every day. But often we take these blessings for granted.

Can you see? You are blessed! Imagine what it is like to be blind. Everyday you look at a thousand things, but when is the last time you thanked God for giving you sight? Sight is an incredible blessing, but we often take it for granted. You are blessed! If you can read, you are blessed! If you are not in bed sick, you are blessed! If you have people who care about you, you are blessed! If you are receiving an education and learning to love learning, you are blessed! If someone in your life loves you so much that they want you to learn about God and his Church, you are blessed! If you have clean water to drink, food to eat, and a place to sleep, you are blessed! If you live in a country where there is liberty and justice, you are blessed!

The list goes on and on. You are blessed!

God is blessing you every day in a thousand ways. Some of these blessings you may take for granted because he gives them to you so often, such as air to breathe, water to drink, food to eat, and a bed to sleep in! This is why it is important to take time each day to count our blessings.

The perfect response to God's blessings has two parts:
First, be grateful; second, share your blessings with others.

Just like the leper who returned to praise Jesus at the top of his voice, we too should express our gratitude to God for all his blessings.

Sharing Your Blessings

The second way to respond perfectly to God's blessings is to share the blessings. God blesses you so that you can bless others! There are more ways for you to bless others than there are stars in the sky. You can bless someone by helping him with something. You can bless someone by listening to what she has to say. You can bless your parents by living a good life. That's right! Good children are a great blessing to their parents. You can bless someone by encouraging him to continue when he wants to give up. You can bless someone by praying for her and asking God to watch over her. You can bless someone by helping him become the-best-version-of-himself.

Few things in life will bring you more joy than sharing God's blessings with others. But in order to share your blessings with others, you need to be very clear about one thing: you are blessed!

So when you lay your head on your pillow tonight, whisper quietly, "I am blessed. Thank you, God, for blessing me today. I am blessed."

Show What You Know

True or False

1. __T__ You are on a great journey with God.

2. __F__ You have nothing to be grateful for.

3. __F__ Gratitude is the worst response to any blessing.

4. __T__ God wants you to become the-best-version-of-yourself.

5. __T__ God loves a grateful heart.

Fill in the blank

1. The greatest blessing God has ever given you
   is __life__ .

2. When we count our blessings, we become full of __Gratitude__
   and __Joy__ .

3. The __catholic__ __church__ is the largest and
   most famous family in the world.

4. __Baptism__ is the beginning of your new life in Jesus.

5. __confirmation__ reminds us that in Baptism
   God blessed us with a special mission and filled us with
   the Holy Spirit.

6. You are a member of God's __Famliy__.

7. When God blesses you abundantly, say __Thank you__ in a big way.

8. Every person in every Bible story has a __lesson__ to teach you.

9. I am __blessed__.

10. God blesses you so that you can __bless__ others.

Word Bank

CONFIRMATION   LIFE   JOY   THANK YOU   BLESSED   FAMILY

CATHOLIC CHURCH   BAPTISM   BLESS   GRATITUDE   LESSON

Journal with Jesus

Dear Jesus,

I am so blessed because . . .

_____

_____

_____

_____

_____

_____

_____

_____

Closing Prayer:

One of the most famous prayers is Mary's song of gratitude, called the Magnificat:

> My soul proclaims the greatness of the Lord,
> and my spirit rejoices in God my savior,
> for he has looked with favor on me.
> From now on all generations will call me blessed.
> For the mighty one has done great things for me,
> and holy is his name.

Adapted from Luke 1:46–49

This was just one of the ways Mary showed her enormous gratitude to God. You too can praise God with your gratitude, morning, noon, and night. Let's praise God right now with our own prayer:

> Oh Lord my God, thank you for all the ways you have blessed
> me in the past, all the ways you are blessing me today,
> and all the ways you plan to bless me in the future.
> I know you have great plans for me.
> Help me never to doubt you.

> Amen.

2

The-Best-Version-
of-Yourself

_____

God, our loving Father,
thank you for all the ways you bless me.
Help me to be aware that every person,
place, and adventure I experience is an
opportunity to love you more.
Fill me with a desire to change and to grow,
and give me the grace to become
the-best-version-of-myself in
every moment of every day.

Amen.

Happiness and Free Will

You are blessed! One of the greatest blessings God has given you is the ability to make choices. We call this free will.

Free will is the gift God gives us to allow us to make our own choices. Each time we make a choice, God hopes we will choose what is good and right and what helps us become the-best-version-of-ourselves.

God has given you free will and he wants you to become a great decision maker. You are young and it might seem like people are always telling you what to do. But you exercise your free will in a hundred ways every day. What are some of the ways you have exercised your free will this week?

God wants to teach you how to make great decisions and do the right thing because he wants you to be happy.

Doing the right thing is also one of the ways we show that we love God, others, and ourselves. God wants your love to be large and generous. He wants you to be kind, loving, thoughtful, compassionate, helpful, and accepting.

Learn to say yes with God. This means that before you say yes to anything, ask yourself: Would God want me to say yes to this? Will this help me become the-best-version-of-myself?

Learn to say no with God too. Before you say no to anything, ask yourself: Would God want me to say no to this?

Say yes with God and say no with God, and your love of God and neighbor will be large and generous. This is the path to happiness.

Making Decisions

One of the most practical skills you can develop in life is to become a great decision maker. King Solomon was called "Solomon the Wise" because he was a great decision maker.

Solomon was just twelve years old when he became king, and he was very nervous about how he would make all the decisions a king needs to make. One night God appeared to Solomon in a dream. He told Solomon he would give him anything he asked for. Solomon asked God for wisdom.

God wants you to become a great decision maker too.

We have spoken about how God wants you to become the-best-version-of-yourself and live a holy life. This is simply not possible unless you get really good at making decisions.

Remember, God doesn't expect you to become wise and learn to make great decisions all on your own. He gives you guidance. One way God guides us is by giving us laws. God gives us directions to follow, which are designed to help us live happy and holy lives by guiding us to make great decisions.

The Best Way to Live

Moses was a great leader chosen by God to lead the Israelites out of slavery in Egypt. The Israelites were God's chosen people, and he blessed them by taking care of them.

God helped the Israelites escape from slavery in Egypt by parting the Red Sea. When the people were hungry, he sent them special food from heaven called manna. When they were thirsty, he made water come out of a rock for them to drink. And God led them to the Promised Land, a fabulous country filled with food and fresh water, where they could all live together as an extended family.

But along the way, the people became restless and ungrateful, began complaining, and turned their backs on God in lots of ways. They were also arguing with each other about what was the best way to live.

And yet, God did not give up on his people. Even though they had turned their backs on him and sinned against him, and even though they were not being the-best-version-of-themselves, he gave them another chance.

God Speaks to Moses

God invited Moses to come up a very high mountain as a representative of the people. On top of Mount Sinai he spoke to Moses through the burning bush. He also gave Moses his law written on two stone tablets—the Ten Commandments.

The Ten Commandments are a blessing from God given to his people. They help us become the-best-version-of-ourselves, grow in virtue, and live holy lives.

The Ten Commandments

The Ten Commandments show us the best way to live, and they are just as important today as they were thousands of years ago when Moses brought them down from Mount Sinai. They point us along the path of wisdom, and lead all of humanity toward peace, harmony, joy, and holiness.

We are always happier when we walk in God's ways. We are always happier when we obey God's laws.

What are the Ten Commandments?

1. I am the Lord your God; you shall not have strange gods before me.

2. You shall not take the name of the Lord your God in vain.

3. Remember to keep holy the Lord's Day.

4. Honor your father and mother.

5. You shall not kill.

6. You shall not commit adultery.

7. You shall not steal.

8. You shall not bear false witness against your neighbor.

9. You shall not covet your neighbor's wife.

10. You shall not covet your neighbor's goods.

Which commandment is the hardest for you to keep?

The Greatest Commandment

Moses lived more than one thousand years before Jesus was born. After he came down from the mountain the people tried to walk with God and live holy lives by obeying his commandments. Some days they did a great job, and other days they gave in to temptation and sin.

As the years passed, more and more of the people turned their backs on God and his law. They stopped trying to live holy lives, became confused about the best way to live, and made excuses for their behavior.

But God still loved his people. So when the time was right, he sent his only son, Jesus, to save people from their sin and confusion and show them the best way to live.

One day Jesus was in the synagogue listening and teaching, when someone asked him a question: "Teacher, which is the greatest of the commandments?" Jesus replied, "You shall love the Lord your God with all your heart, with all your soul, and with all your mind. This is the greatest commandment. And the second is like it: "You shall love your neighbor as yourself" (Matthew 22:36–40).

Love One Another

If we love God with all our hearts, souls, and minds, we will try every day to become a-better-version-of-ourselves, to live holy lives, and obey God's commandments.

Jesus wanted everyone to know that it is not enough just to say that we love God. He wanted us to know that one of the most powerful ways we show God that we love him is by loving other people. Jesus was always standing up for the people who could not stand up for themselves. And he teaches us to treat other people the way we would like to be treated.

God is constantly trying to show us the best way to live. He gave Moses the Ten Commandments to share with us so that we could live holy lives. He sent Jesus to clear the confusion about what is right and what is wrong. After Jesus died, rose from the dead, and ascended into heaven, God the Father sent the Holy Spirit to guide us. He has also given us the Bible and the One, Holy, Catholic, and Apostolic Church to help us answer all the questions we have along the way.

Remember, you are on a journey with God. Along the way you are going to have lots of questions. That's okay. Everyone has questions in their journey with God. A little later we will talk about what to do when you don't know what to do.

Temptation, Sin, and Grace

Even though God is constantly trying to show us the best way to live, we are tempted from time to time to wander away from his path.

What is temptation? Temptation is the desire to do something that is unwise or wrong.

We experience temptation in a hundred ways. Sometimes temptation comes in the form of thoughts.

We might think, "Maybe I should copy my friends homework and then I won't have to do it myself." Sometimes our friends lead us into temptation. One of them might say, "Let's go down to the park without telling our parents." And sometimes we lead other people into temptation by suggesting things that don't help them become the-best-version-of-themselves.

In our hearts we know these things are wrong. When was the last time you were tempted to do something that you knew was wrong?

Overcoming Temptation

The best way to deal with temptation is to turn to God in prayer and ask him for his help.

Prayer is a conversation with God. Prayer isn't just something we do before meals, or at church on Sunday, or before we go to bed at night. These are all important ways to pray, but God wants you to talk to him throughout the day. At any moment of the day, if you have to make a decision, that's a great time to turn to God in prayer. Ask him to guide you to make the best decision.

God always wants to help you make the right decision. He has given you free will so that you can say yes or no to things, but he wants to help you use your free will to make good and wise decisions. Above all, God has given you free will so that you can love.

Some decisions you make help you become the-best-version-of-yourself, and some do not. Some decisions you make help other people become the-best-version-of-themselves, and some do not. God always wants to help you become the-very-best-version-of-yourself, and to help others become all he created them to be too.

Let's look together at an example.

You are taking a test and you don't know the answer to a question. You may be tempted to cheat by looking at someone else's answer. But cheating won't help you become the-best-version-of-yourself.

Let's pray together right now about temptation.

> **Lord, anytime I feel tempted**
> **to do something that is wrong**
> **and doesn't help me become**
> **the-best-version-of-myself,**
> **please inspire me to choose**
> **what is good and right.**
>
> **Amen.**

What Is Sin?

God has a marvelous plan for you and your life. As a loving Father, he wants you to become the-best-version-of-yourself by living a holy life.

Sometimes when you are thinking about making a choice that you know you should not make, you get this gnawing, yucky feeling in the pit of your stomach. That feeling is the-best-version-of-yourself, or your conscience, saying, "No, no, no! Don't do it! This is not a good choice for you!"

Sometimes you listen to that voice, and you stop and make a better choice. But at other times, you might continue on and make the bad choice anyway. What happens to that yucky feeling in your belly? It just gets worse because . . . you've sinned against God!

When you have purposely made a poor choice, you have sinned. When you sin you break God's commandments by choosing an action that turns away from him. Some sins hurt our relationship with God; these are called venial sins. Other sins break our relationship with God; these are called mortal sins.

God's Grace

Not everything that makes us feel embarrassed or ashamed is a sin. Mistakes and accidents can make us feel this way too. Let's have a look at an example together.

Perhaps you knock over your milk at breakfast. This is an accident, not a sin. Or maybe you trip over your little sister's toy and break it. This is an accident, not a sin. Maybe you get the answers wrong on your math test or spelling test. This is a mistake, not a sin.

Accidents and mistakes happen. What God wants is for us to avoid intentional sin by making great choices and keeping his commandments.

The best way to deal with sin is to go to Reconciliation. When your body gets sick, you go to the doctor and he or she helps you get better. When your soul gets sick because of sin, you go to Reconciliation and the priest helps you get better.

Through Reconciliation God forgives our sins, but he also gives us grace to help us avoid sin in the future.

What is grace? Grace is the help God gives us to do what is good and right.

God's grace helps us to become the-best-version-of-ourselves. God's grace helps us to grow in virtue. God's grace helps us to live holy lives. God's grace helps us to have healthy relationships. God's grace allows us to share in his life and love.

From the Bible: Adam and Eve

Sometimes we use our free will in ways that are good, and sometimes we use it in ways that hurt ourselves and others. This is something the first human beings discovered. Who were the first human beings?

Adam and Eve.

God loved Adam and Eve so much that he blessed them with free will. He gave them a beautiful world to live in and they had everything they needed.

Because he loved them so much, he warned them, "Do not eat the fruit of the tree in the middle of the garden because, if you do, you will die!"

It's important to understand that the reason God didn't want them to eat the fruit was because he loved them so much and didn't want them to hurt themselves.

One day Adam and Eve were in the middle of the garden, near the forbidden tree with the forbidden fruit.

A snake came along and started talking to them. Then the snake said, "You should eat the fruit."

"Oh, we can't," Eve said.

"Why not?" asked the snake.

"If we eat it we will die!" Eve explained.

"No you won't," said the snake.

At that moment Adam and Eve began to doubt all the good things that God had done for them and told them.

Then Eve took the fruit and ate it. She gave some to Adam and he ate it too.

All at once they realized they had made a terrible mistake, and it made them sad. This is the story of original sin and temptation. Original means "first" (adapted from Genesis 3:1–7).

Adam and Eve experienced temptation and sin, and so do you and I. They made a bad decision. God wants to teach you how to be a great decision maker so you can live a rich, full, happy life in this world— and live with him in heaven in eternal bliss forever.

Follow Your Conscience

We have been exploring some of the many ways God has blessed you. Life is the greatest blessing. Free will is another fabulous blessing. Both come with great responsibility.

To help you become the-best-version-of-yourself and live a holy life, God has also blessed you with a conscience. Conscience is the gentle voice inside you that encourages you to do good and avoid evil. God speaks to us through our conscience. Your conscience encourages you to become the-best-version-of-yourself. It also warns you when you are thinking of doing something that will offend God and make you unhappy.

The more we listen to our conscience and obey what it tells us, the easier it becomes to hear it. At first it may be difficult to follow our conscience. Lots of things are difficult at first. But don't give up. Keep trying. Never stop trying. God will never give up on you, and you should never give up on yourself.

Following our conscience makes us happy. Ignoring our conscience makes us restless and unhappy.

Do you know what a regret is? A regret is something you wish you had not done. All our regrets come from ignoring our conscience.

Sometimes you are thinking of doing something, but you get a yucky feeling inside or you hear a little voice inside you advising you not to do it. That is your conscience. If you do that thing and ignore your conscience, that yucky feeling will sink deep down into your heart and soul. But if you listen to that gentle voice inside you and do the right thing, you will be glad you did and filled with joy.

Follow your conscience. You will never regret it.

When You Don't Know What to Do

There will be times in our lives when we are not sure what to do. When you are faced with a decision and you are unsure what to do, here are some tips to help you make a great decision.

1. Find a quiet place and spend a few minutes listening to your conscience. Ask yourself: What is my conscience encouraging me to do?

2. Think about the Ten Commandments. Ask yourself: Do the Ten Commandments help me see clearly what I should do in this situation?

3. Ask your parents, priest, catechist, or teacher for advice.

4. Pray to the Holy Spirit and ask him to help you make the best decision.

Nobody is perfect. There will be times when you turn your back on God and his way of doing things. There will be times when you abandon the-best-version-of-yourself. There will be times when you live a selfish life rather than a holy life.

When that happens, recognize it. Don't get discouraged. Go to Reconciliation and start over again. Our God is a God of second chances. Praise be to God! We all need another chance every now and then, and God is always willing to give us another chance and a fresh start. That's just one of the many good reasons why God gives us the incredible gift of Reconciliation.

Show What You Know

True or False

1. __T__ We are always happier when we walk in God's ways.

2. __F__ If we love God with all our hearts, souls, and minds we won't listen to him.

3. __F__ One of the most powerful ways we show God we love him is by being mean to other people.

4. __T__ God is constantly trying to show us the best way to live.

5. __T__ God has a marvelous plan for you and your life.

Fill in the blank

1. God wants you to become a great __decinonmaker__.

2. One of the greatest blessings God has given you is the ability to make __choices__.

3. God loves you so much that he blesses you with __Free will__ __Will__.

4. The best way to deal with sin is to go to __Reconiliation__.

5. By guiding us to make great decisions, God's laws are designed to help us live __Happy__ and __Holy__ lives.

6. The path to happiness begins with saying _Yes_ with God and _no_ with God.

7. The best way to deal with temptation is to turn to God in _Prayer_ and ask him for his help.

8. Following our conscience makes us _happy_ and ignoring our conscience makes us restless and _unHaPPy_.

9. God's _Grace_ helps us to become the-best-version-of-ourselves.

10. Our God is a God of _Second_ chances.

Word Bank

~~PRAYER~~	~~HOLY~~
~~HAPPY~~	~~FREE WILL~~
~~YES~~	~~NO~~
~~GRACE~~	~~RECONCILIATION~~
~~DECISION MAKER~~	~~CHOICES~~
~~SECOND~~	~~UNHAPPY~~
~~HAPPY~~	

Journal with Jesus

Dear Jesus,

I am the-best-version-of-myself when I . . .

_____

_____

_____

_____

_____

_____

_____

_____

Closing Prayer

Throughout the Bible we read about angels helping people. There are three Archangels whom God has given great power to. Their names are Michael, Gabriel, and Raphael. The Church also teaches that God has appointed an angel for every person—including you. We call this angel your Guardian Angel.

Your Guardian Angel is there to guide and protect you. The Church invites us to pray this special prayer to our Guardian Angel:

> **Angel of God,**
> **my Guardian dear,**
> **to whom God's love commits me here,**
> **ever this day be at my side,**
> **to light and guard, to rule and guide**.
>
> **Amen**.

This is a great prayer to begin the day with. It also is a great prayer to pray when we are afraid. You may even want to name your Guardian Angel, so you can speak with him or her throughout the day.

3

God Sent Jesus to Save Us

———————

God, our loving Father,
thank you for all the ways you bless me.
Help me to be aware that every person,
place, and adventure I experience is an
opportunity to love you more.
Fill me with a desire to change and to grow,
and give me the grace to become
the-best-version-of-myself in
every moment of every day.

Amen.

The Mess

Since the beginning, human beings have been trying to figure out the best way to live. God often sent great prophets to lead and guide the people, but many of the people didn't listen to them. Finally, when the time was just right, God sent his only Son, Jesus.

The world was a mess because people were confused about who they were and the purpose of life. They were lost. They needed to be saved from their selfishness and sin.

So God sent his Son, Jesus, to save them. And he didn't send Jesus just for the people of that time; he sent Jesus to save the people of all times. Do you need to be saved from your selfishness?

You see, your story and Jesus' story are connected. Jesus' story is not just about what happened two thousand years ago. It is also about your friendship with him today.

We all need to be saved, and people who need to be saved need a savior. Jesus is the Savior of the world. What does that mean?

We All Need Saving

Imagine you went into a store and ate an ice cream, even though you didn't have the money to pay for it. This would be wrong and illegal, and the storeowner would have every right to be very angry with you and call the police. But just at that moment a friend of yours comes into the store, realizes what is happening, and gives his own money to the store owner to pay for the ice cream you stole. Your friend has paid your debt. In this situation, your friend has saved you.

Another example would be if you went swimming at the beach and got caught in the current and carried out to sea. As the waves get bigger and you become tired, you start drowning.

But just at that moment a lifeguard comes along in a rescue boat and brings you safely back to shore. The lifeguard has saved you.

Jesus is Your Savior

Now, think about all the men, women, and children since the beginning of time, and the many things that they have done that are selfish and wrong and offend God. Jesus came and paid the price for all of these sins by dying for you and me on the cross. Why? Because he wants you to be happy with him forever in heaven. Amazing, isn't it? When Jesus was on the cross, he thought of you. He loved you then and he loves you now.

Many people can save you from various situations, but only Jesus can save you from your sins.

Jesus' Birth & Childhood

Jesus had a huge mission: to save every sinner in history from their sins. That's a big mission, right?

And yet, God in his wisdom decided not to come as the king of a great nation or as a powerful political leader. He didn't even come as the son of a rich man, but as a baby born in a stable.

What lesson does this teach us? God's ways are not man's ways.

God has a unique way of doing things. He has wisdom far beyond that of the wisest men and women in this world. His ways are far superior to our own ways. He has a better plan for your life than any you could dream up for yourself. Ask God to fill you with his wisdom so that you can learn his way of doing things.

God came into the world as a tiny, helpless child. Every year we celebrate the miracle of Jesus' birth. Christmas is Jesus' birthday. But if Christmas is Jesus' birthday, why do you get presents?

The Quiet Years

After Jesus' birth, we know very little about the next thirty years of his life. What do you think he was doing?

Everything would suggest that Jesus lived a very normal life. His daily routines would have been very similar to those of other boys and girls he grew up with.

We do catch a glimpse of Jesus' childhood when he was traveling with Mary and Joseph to Jerusalem. During this trip Jesus got separated from his parents. Eventually they found him in the Temple.

Have you ever lost something important and then found it again? What did it feel like when you realized you had lost it? How did you feel when you found it? How do you think Mary and Joseph felt when they could not find Jesus?

Jesus' Ministry

The next we hear about Jesus is at the wedding in Cana. They ran out of wine and Mary asked Jesus to help. So Jesus asked the servants to fill six large jars with water and Jesus transformed the water into wine. This was his first miracle.

No doubt word quickly spread about this miracle, which would have made it very difficult for Jesus to return to a normal life. This was the beginning of Jesus' public life, during which he made his way around the region teaching and healing many people.

Jesus was fully divine, but he was also fully human. He loved the everyday aspects of life as a human being. We often see him enjoying a meal with friends and strangers. Here we see him celebrating at a wedding. Jesus loved life.

The Disciples

One of the things Jesus loved about life was friendship. At the beginning of his ministry, he surrounded himself with twelve disciples. He personally invited each of them to follow him. He knew that he was going to die to bring salvation to all humanity, and that others would be needed to carry on the mission.

In every place and in every time, Jesus calls men, women, and children to follow him and carry on his mission. He invites you to become one of his disciples in the world today.

How can you carry on Jesus' mission?

Jesus' Parables

Throughout his public life Jesus used parables to share his wisdom with ordinary people. These parables were easy for ordinary people to understand because they were based on examples from everyday life.

Jesus taught in this way because the religious leaders of his time had made everything very complicated. Jesus wanted ordinary people to be able to understand his message and make their way to God. He taught us that there is genius in simplicity. One of the most difficult things in the world to do is to take something that is complex and make it simple.

Which parable is your favorite?

The Miracles of Jesus

Jesus performed hundreds of miracles. He healed the sick, made the blind see and the lame walk, and comforted the afflicted. He didn't do these things to show off or amaze people. Jesus performed miracles because he felt tremendous mercy for people and wanted to demonstrate the awesome compassion he had for those who were struggling and suffering. He also wanted people to be absolutely clear that he was not just a great teacher, but that he was God.

God has great compassion for his people. One of the ways we can share in Jesus' mission is by bringing his compassion to everyone who crosses our path in life.

If you could perform one of Jesus' miracles today, which would you choose? Why?

The Cross, Resurrection, and Ascension

Most people thought it was just another Friday, but it wasn't. We call the day Jesus died on the cross Good Friday because it was the day that Jesus saved us from our sins and repaired our relationship with God. On that day Jesus was beaten, bullied, mocked, spat upon, cursed at, and crucified on the cross. Jesus knew all this would happen, and he let it happen anyway, because he loved us so much that he was willing to lay down his life for us.

God loves you so much. He will go to unimaginable lengths to prove his love for you.

The Resurrection

On Sunday morning, three days after Jesus died on the cross, he rose from the dead. We call this the Resurrection. Never before and never since has anyone raised himself from the dead.

The Resurrection is the most important event in history.

One of the reasons that Jesus died on the cross and rose from the dead was so that we could go to heaven. God wants you to live with him and the angels and saints in heaven forever.

Do you want to go to heaven? Why?

The Ascension

For forty days after he rose from the dead, Jesus appeared to many people. Then he took the eleven remaining disciples out to a place near Bethany. He blessed them and then ascended into heaven, forty days after the Resurrection.

We call this the Ascension.

Jesus is a bridge between heaven and earth. By ascending into heaven he cleared the way for us to receive the ultimate blessing: eternal life.

You are blessed.

Why were there only eleven disciples at the Ascension?

From the Bible: Pentecost

Before Jesus left the disciples to ascend into heaven he promised to send the Holy Spirit to help them live good lives and carry out their mission. Jesus makes that same promise to you. He promised to send the Holy Spirit to guide you so you can make great decisions, become the-best-version-of-yourself, live a holy life, and help other people experience God's love.

At Pentecost Jesus kept his promise.

After Jesus died on the cross, rose from the dead, and ascended into heaven, many people were angry at his disciples. The disciples were afraid of what the angry people might do to them.

One day they were all gathered together in an upper room when they heard a loud sound like a howling wind. Then the Holy Spirit descended upon them and filled them with the wisdom and courage they needed to carry out the mission Jesus had entrusted to them.

When you were baptized the Holy Spirit came upon you, and when you get confirmed the gifts of the Holy Spirit will be strengthened in you. This will allow you to continue Jesus' mission in your own way.

Before the Holy Spirit came the disciples were afraid. After they received the Holy Spirit they were filled with courage, and they went out and changed the world. If you are ever afraid, ask the Holy Spirit to fill you with courage.

There are many things that we cannot do on our own, but with God's grace and the power of the Holy Spirit we can do great things.

You and the Church

Pentecost is the birthday of the Church. We celebrate Pentecost every year, just like you celebrate your birthday.

Jesus gave us the Church to pass his message on to the people of every place and every time. On Sunday at Mass Jesus' message is passed on to you and your family.

The Church also passes along the Sacraments, so that you can continue to receive the grace you need to become the-best-version-of-youself, grow in virtue, and live a holy life.

You are blessed to be a member of the One, Holy, Catholic, and Apostolic Church.

How do you think it would have been different being a Christian two thousand years ago than it is today?

You

Jesus' story doesn't stop there. In fact, for you Jesus' story is just beginning. He wants you to be part of his story.

It's real. Just like the lepers, the prodigal son, the woman at the well, and the disciples, Jesus wants you to be part of his story. And he wants to be part of your story too.

If you could be any person in the Jesus story, who would you be?

The Jesus story never ends. It is unfolding here, today, right now. And Jesus wants you to be a part of the story.

You are blessed to be part of the story. The mess of the world can make us sad at times, but Jesus wants us to be supremely happy. He invites us to have a dynamic and personal relationship with him so that he can share his happiness with us and we can share it with others.

So, each morning when you wake up and each night before you go to bed, take a minute to talk to Jesus.

Show What You Know

True or False

1. _____ When Jesus was on the cross, he thought of you because he loves you.

2. _____ Jesus wants you to become one of his disciples.

3. _____ You are blessed to be a member of the Catholic Church.

4. _____ The Sacraments help make you the-worst-version-of-yourself.

5. _____ Jesus wants you to be a part of his story.

Fill in the blank

1. Jesus _____ life.

2. It takes _____ to be able to see God's ways and walk in them.

3. Jesus wanted _____ people to be able to understand his message and make their way to God.

4. God will go to unimaginable lengths to prove his _____ for you.

5. Jesus performed miracles because he felt tremendous _____ for people.

6. The _____ is the most important event in history.

7. God wants you to live with him and the angels and saints in

   _____ forever.

8. Jesus is a _____ between heaven and earth.

9. With God's grace and the power of the _____

   _____ we can do great things.

10. Jesus invites you to have a _____ and

    _____ relationship with him so that he can share

    his happiness with us and we can share it with others.

Word Bank

LOVE	DYNAMIC	HOLY SPIRIT	WISDOM	HEAVEN	MERCY
LOVES	PERSONAL	ORDINARY	BRIDGE	RESURRECTION	

Journal with Jesus

Dear Jesus,

Learning about your life teaches me . . .

_____

_____

_____

_____

_____

_____

_____

_____

Closing Prayer

Jesus said, "Ask and you shall receive" (Matthew 7:7). There are going to be times in your life when you don't know what to do. That's a great time to turn to the Holy Spirit and ask for insight. There are going to be times in your life when you need encouragement. The Holy Spirit is the great encourager. Turn to him and ask him to encourage you. There are going to be times in your life when you are afraid. Ask the Holy Spirit to give you courage. There are going to be times in your life when you don't know what to say. Turn to the Holy Spirit and ask him to give you the words.

We all have a daily need for the Holy Spirit. As we grow older we become less dependent on some people and some things, but we always need the Holy Spirit's guidance.

Saint Augustine wandered far away from God when he was young, but then he went to Reconciliation, turned back to God, and ultimately became a great priest and bishop.

Let's pray his prayer to the Holy Spirit together:

> **Breathe into me, Holy Spirit, that my thoughts may all be holy.**
> **Move in me, Holy Spirit, that my work, too, may be holy.**
> **Attract my heart, Holy Spirit, that I may love only what is holy.**
> **Strengthen me, Holy Spirit, that I may defend all that is holy.**
> **Protect me, Holy Spirit, that I may always be holy.**
>
> **Amen.**

4
Forgiveness and Healing

God, our loving Father,
thank you for all the ways you bless me.
Help me to be aware that every person,
place, and adventure I experience is an
opportunity to love you more.
Fill me with a desire to change and to grow,
and give me the grace to become
the-best-version-of-myself in
every moment of every day.

Amen.

God Loves Healthy Relationships

God loves relationships. He delights in his relationship with you, and he delights in your healthy relationships with others.

God is a perfect friend because he always helps you become the-best-version-of-yourself. Other people might ask you to do things that will lead you to become a-second-rate-version-of-yourself, but not God. Everything he asks you to do comes from his desire for you to become the-best-version-of-yourself, live a holy life, and be happy.

Forgiveness is essential to healthy relationships. Two of the most important life lessons are how to forgive and how to be forgiven. These two lessons are part of the Our Father prayer. We pray, "Forgive us our trespasses as we forgive those who trespass against us." We are saying sorry to God for any wrong we have done and asking him to give us the grace to forgive anyone who has wronged us.

Forgiveness

Have you ever done something that you knew was wrong?
How did it make you feel?

We all mess up and make bad choices sometimes. Saint Paul
teaches us that we have all sinned and fallen short of God's dreams
for us. These are just some of the reasons that God blesses us with
the Sacrament of Reconciliation.

When was the last time you forgave someone? When was the last time someone forgave you?

We don't talk about forgiveness to blame ourselves or to feel bad about ourselves. God doesn't want that. We talk about these things so we can do something about them.

Max and His Room

Here's a story to help us all understand. One day Max got his very own bedroom. Everything was perfect and in its place. But the next day, after church, Max threw his nice church clothes on the floor as he got changed to go outside and play with his friends. He didn't realize it at the time, but this was the beginning of a growing problem.

The next day Max threw his pajamas on the floor instead of putting them where they belong. That afternoon after soccer he left his soccer gear on the floor in the middle of the room. The following day he had some potato chips and a candy bar, but instead of putting the wrappers in the trash can, he threw them on the floor.

This went on for three weeks. Max just kept throwing things where they didn't belong.

Then one day he came home and he couldn't open the door to his room. He went looking for his mother and asked, "Mom, why did you lock my room?"

"I didn't lock your room," his mom said.

"Well, I can't get in there. Someone must have locked it."

Max's mom tried to get in the room, but she couldn't. "Maybe something is blocking the door," she said.

Max and his mother went outside and looked in the window to see what was blocking the door. They were amazed at what they saw. All of Max's stuff that he had been leaving everywhere for weeks had fallen in front of the door and was blocking him from getting into his room.

When Max's dad came home, he pushed very hard against the door and forced everything to move so Max could climb into his room.

Max spent four hours putting everything away in the right places. He put his clothes in his closet or hamper, he put all his toys away, and he put anything that was trash in the trash can.

When he was finished he promised never to let his room get so messy again.

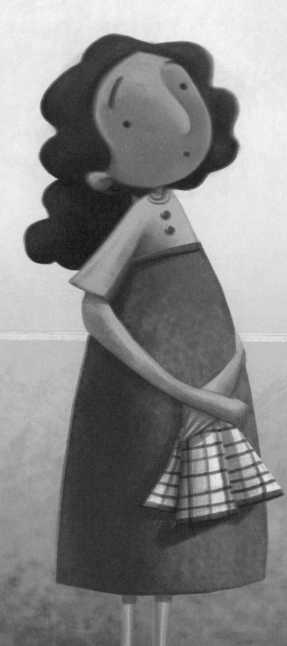

Just as Max made a mess of his room, sometimes we make a mess in our souls. We leave little sins lying around here and there, and before you know it, they are piling up.

Jesus wants to work with you to tidy up your soul. That's what he is going to do during your First Reconciliation.

What Is a Sacrament?

A Sacrament is a celebration of God's love for humanity. Through the Sacraments God fills us with the grace we need to become the-best-version-of-ourselves, grow in virtue, and live holy lives.

It is not easy to become the-best-version-of-yourself.

It is not easy to grow in virtue.

It is not easy to live a holy life.

We need God's help. We need God's grace, and the first step is to know that we need it.

Imagine making a journey from New York to San Francisco. You start out walking. It's not difficult to walk down the street, but it's difficult to walk almost three thousand miles from New York to San Francisco.

After a couple of days walking, you think to yourself, "I need a bike." But after a couple of days riding the bike, that doesn't seem so great anymore either. You keep riding and then your parish priest comes along side you and says, "Rachel, what you need is a bus." Along comes a bus and you jump on. It turns out that Jesus is driving the bus. He says, "Hi Rachel, I'm going to help you get there."

The Sacraments and the grace we receive through them are like Jesus' bus. They help us get where we need to go—not to San Francisco, but to heaven.

What Is Reconciliation?

Well, first, Reconciliation is a Sacrament. So it's one of the ways God blesses us with the grace to become the-best-version-of-ourselves, grow in virtue, and live holy lives.

In particular, Reconciliation is an opportunity to talk to God about the times we have messed up, made poor choices, not been the-best-version-of-ourselves, or turned our backs on God and his wonderful plans for us.

Reconciliation is an opportunity for us to say sorry to him and ask for forgiveness.

It is also an opportunity for the priest to share some ideas about how we can do better in the future. It's like when your coach gives you some tips at halftime about how you can do better. Our priest is one of our spiritual coaches. Great champions listen to their coaches.

We all mess up, and those things can weigh us down. If we don't go to Reconciliation our hearts can become heavy. Through the Sacrament of Reconciliation God forgives our sins and takes the weight of those things off our hearts, so we can live with joy— and share his joy with others.

From the Bible: Our Father

You are the son or daughter of a great King. God is that great King. Jesus wanted you to know this. Over and over throughout his life he reminded us that we are children of God.

The disciples often saw Jesus go off to a quiet place to pray. They were curious about prayer and they asked him to teach them how to pray (Matthew 6:9–13).

Jesus taught them to say:

Our Father
Who art in heaven
Hallowed be thy name.
Thy kingdom come,
Thy will be done
On earth as it is in heaven.
Give us this day our daily bread
And forgive us our trespasses.
As we forgive those who trespass against us,
And lead us not into temptation,
But deliver us from evil.

Amen.

Each morning when you wake up, start your day by praying the Our Father. Each night before you go to sleep, end your day by praying the Our Father.

You Are Blessed

You are the son or daughter of a great King. Jesus wanted us to always remember that God is our Father and that we are children of God.

Now let's say this together:

I am blessed. I am the daughter/son of a great King. He is my Father and my God. The world may praise me or criticize me. It matters not. He is with me, always at my side, guiding and protecting me. I do not fear because I am his.

The Good Shepherd

Jesus loved to share his wisdom with people by telling stories. One of the stories he told was about a shepherd.

The shepherd had one hundred sheep, and he loved every single one of them and took very good care of them. He made sure they had plenty of food and water, and when the wild wolves came he chased them away from his sheep.

One day one of the sheep got lost. He counted his sheep but only got to ninety-nine. The shepherd was very sad.

So he went out looking for the lost sheep. He looked down by the stream and up in the mountains. Then finally, he heard the sheep crying. It had caught its foot in some wire and couldn't get free.

The shepherd carefully removed the sheep's foot from the wire, then picked the sheep up in his arms and carried it all the way home. He was filled with joy that he had found the lost sheep, and he rejoiced.

The shepherd was a very good shepherd. He loved his sheep, and his sheep loved him.

Jesus is the Good Shepherd and we are his sheep. He wants to take care of us. He doesn't want any of us to get lost, but if we do he comes searching for us to save us and bring us home.

Jesus wants to lead us to the home that God the Father has prepared for us in heaven.

Adapted from John 10:1—21

God Will Always Love You

Like the sheep in the story, we all wander astray from time to time. When we do, it is good to go to Reconciliation and say sorry.

Sometimes when we do the wrong thing we may be tempted to think that some people will not like us anymore. We may even be tempted to think that God will not love us anymore. But that is never true.

God will always love you. There is nothing you can do that will make him stop loving you. We all make mistakes, we all mess up, and we all make poor choices from time to time. But God never stops loving us. You need to always remember this.

You may think you have done something horrible and God will never forgive you. But that is stinking thinking. God doesn't want you to think like that. He is always willing to forgive us when we are sorry, and there is nothing you can do that will cause him to stop loving you.

God loves you so much. He loves you so much that he wants to help you every day and in every way to become the-best-version-of-yourself!

Show What You Know

True or False

1. _____ Forgiveness is essential to healthy relationships.

2. _____ God doesn't forgive us.

3. _____ God gives us confession so we can feel bad about ourselves.

4. _____ Your priest is one of your spiritual coaches.

5. _____ God is always willing to forgive you.

Fill in the blank

1. God delights in a healthy _____ with you and others.

2. God invites you to become the-best-version-of-yourself because he wants you to live a holy life and be _____.

3. In relationships two of the most important life lessons are: how to _____ and how to be _____.

4. In the _____ _____ we pray, "forgive us our trespasses as we forgive those who trespass against us."

5. Because we all sin, God blesses us with the Sacrament of _____ so we can live with joy and share his joy with others.

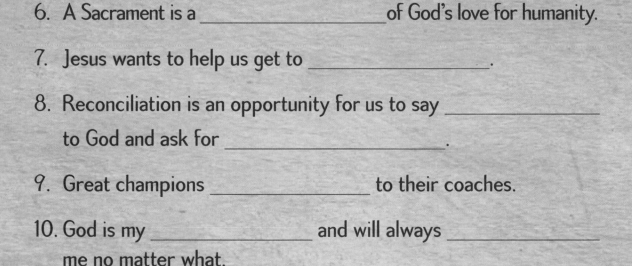

6. A Sacrament is a _____ of God's love for humanity.

7. Jesus wants to help us get to _____.

8. Reconciliation is an opportunity for us to say _____ to God and ask for _____.

9. Great champions _____ to their coaches.

10. God is my _____ and will always _____ me no matter what.

Word Bank

LOVE   FORGIVE   LISTEN   SORRY   FATHER   FORGIVEN   RECONCILIATION

HAPPY   HEAVEN   FORGIVENESS   RELATIONSHIP   OUR FATHER   CELEBRATION

Journal with Jesus

Dear Jesus,

I know you will always love me because . . .

_____

_____

_____

_____

_____

_____

_____

Closing Prayer

Since the beginning of time, God has been using ordinary people to accomplish extraordinary things. King David is just one example. He came from a big family, and as a child he worked in the fields as a shepherd boy.

One day David brought lunch to his seven brothers who were on the battlefield defending Israel against the Philistines. David arrived and heard the giant Goliath making fun of the Israelites and God. Goliath was the Philistines' greatest warrior and he thought he was more powerful than God. Everyone was afraid of Goliath and refused to fight him.

Believing in the power of God's protection, David volunteered to fight Goliath. God gave David great courage and helped him to slay Goliath. No one believed that young David could defeat the great warrior Goliath. But anything is possible with God.

Later in his life, after King Saul died, David became King of Israel. Until Jesus, David was the greatest king in Israel's history. But David was not perfect. When David made himself available to God great things happened. When he closed himself off to God his life started to fall apart. With God he was happy. When he turned away from God he was miserable.

Adapted from 1 Samuel 17 and 2 Samuel 4–5

King David recognized these patterns of happiness and misery in his life. He learned that when he allowed God to lead him, like he used to lead the sheep in the pastures as a child, he was happiest. With this wisdom he wrote one of the most famous prayers of all time. It is called Psalm 23:

> **The Lord is my shepherd, there is nothing I shall want;**
> **he lets me lay down in green pastures.**
> **He leads me beside peaceful waters;**
> **he restores my soul.**
> **He leads me in paths of righteousness for his name's sake.**
> **Even though I walk through the valley of the shadow of death,**
> **I will not be afraid; for he is with me;**
> **his rod and his staff, they comfort and protect me.**
> **He prepares a table before me in the presence of my enemies;**
> **he anoints my head with oil, my cup overflows.**
> **Surely goodness and mercy will follow me all the days of my life;**
> **and I will live in the house of the Lord forever.**
>
> **Amen.**

5

Your First Reconciliation

God, our loving Father,
thank you for all the ways you bless me.
Help me to be aware that every person,
place, and adventure I experience is an
opportunity to love you more.
Fill me with a desire to change and to grow,
and give me the grace to become
the-best-version-of-myself in
every moment of every day.

Amen.

Great Moments in Life

Life is full of great moments. When you were born, that was a great moment. Christmas, Easter, feast days, and birthdays are all great moments.

The first time you score a goal in soccer is a great moment. The day you graduate from college is a great moment. Getting your first job is a great moment. Discovering your vocation is a great moment.

Ordinary moments can be great too—like a beautiful sunset, a fabulous meal with family, or meeting a new friend.

Your First Reconciliation is going to be one of the great moments of your life.

The Garden of Your Heart

Imagine you are in a beautiful garden. It is springtime and the grass is green, the sun is shining, the flowers are blossoming with bright colors, butterflies are fluttering, bees are buzzing, and the birds are happily chirping.

Then you notice some nasty weeds and overgrown thornbushes over by the edge of the garden.

Now the gardener comes. He waters all the flowers, sings with the birds, enjoys the sunshine, and pets a rabbit that hops by. As the gardener makes his way around the garden he notices what you noticed: the nasty weeds and overgrown thornbushes. He doesn't get angry; he just smiles lovingly and gets to work. He carefully pulls out the weeds and removes the thornbushes. Then he tills the soil and plants some seeds so that this area can be as beautiful as the rest of the garden.

The garden in this story is your heart. The beautiful flowers in the garden are the love you carry in your heart for God and for your family and friends.

Every time you make a good choice, the garden becomes even more beautiful. Every time you help a friend or a stranger, a flower blooms. Each time you choose to listen to your parents, the grass gets a little bit greener. But every time you push someone on the playground or cut in front of someone at the drinking fountain, a weed grows in your garden. And each time you tell a lie or say a bad word, the thornbush begins to grow.

Jesus is the gardener. He wants to live in your heart. He loves walking in your garden, enjoying the beauty of your heart. He also wants to remove all the weeds and thornbushes from your garden. The weeds are the small sins; the thornbushes are your big sins. If you don't get rid of the weeds and thornbushes as soon as they start to grow, they can spread very quickly and take over the whole garden.

In the Sacrament of Reconciliation we invite Jesus the gardener to come into the garden of our hearts and remove all the weeds and thornbushes.

Preparation Matters

We prepare for everything important.

You wouldn't expect to win a big soccer tournament if you hadn't been practicing. You cannot expect good grades if you don't study for your exams. You wouldn't go on a trip without packing and planning. Preparation is essential for a great experience.

You are blessed to be Catholic. As Catholics we prepare for each of the Catholic Moments. We prepare for Christmas with the season of Advent. We prepare for Easter with the season of Lent. We prepare for Mass with prayer and fasting.

You have been preparing for your First Reconciliation. As that wonderful day gets closer, there are some final preparations to be made.

The Five Steps

You are preparing for your First Reconciliation. This will be your first time, but not your last time. You are blessed.

The second time you go to Reconciliation you will know what to do because you will have done it before. But because this is your first time, it makes sense to walk through exactly what will happen.

Let's take a step-by-step look at the Sacrament of Reconciliation so you can know how it works. Then we will talk about each step in detail so you will know what to expect.

First, it is natural to be a little nervous. The first time we do most things we feel nervous. It's like riding a roller coaster: The first time you are really nervous, but the more times you ride it, the less nervous you become.

There are five steps to making a great Reconciliation. Here is a quick overview.

Step 1: Examination of Conscience

This is a spiritual exercise designed to help us remember when we were and when we were not the-best-version-of-ourselves. By examining our conscience we become aware of our sins.

Step 2: Confession

Here we say sorry to God by confessing our sins to him through the priest who is God's representative.

Step 3: Penance

The priest will ask you to spend some time in prayer or to do a kind deed for somebody. This is called penance, which is a way for you to show God that you are truly sorry for your sins.

Step 4: Contrition

The Act of Contrition is a short prayer we pray promising to try not to sin again.

Step 5: Absolution

The priest will then extend his hands over your head and pray a very special and powerful prayer. Acting as God's representative, he will forgive your sins!

Step 1: We Examine Our Conscience

To help you become the-best-version-of-yourself and live a holy life, God has blessed you with a conscience, the gentle voice inside you that encourages you to do good and avoid evil. God speaks to us through our conscience.

Following our conscience makes us happy. Ignoring our conscience makes us irritable, restless, and unhappy.

God doesn't want us to be restless and unhappy, so he gives us the gift of Reconciliation. When we disobey our conscience and sin by doing things that we know we shouldn't do, God invites us to come to Reconciliation so that he can fill us with his joy again.

Before we go to Reconciliation we examine our conscience so that we know what to talk to the priest about. To examine means to look at something very carefully.

Imagine you had a beautiful big diamond and you carried it with you everywhere you went. From time to time you would probably take it out and look at it. If it was very dusty or dirty, you would clean it. If it had a scratch, you would polish it.

Your soul is that beautiful diamond. We come to Reconciliation so God can dust, clean, and polish it so that it can shine like new again.

Before you go to Reconciliation it helps to think back and remember any times that you have chosen to sin, walked down a wrong path, made a poor choice, broken one of God's commandments, not listened to your conscience, or simply not been the-best-version-of-yourself.

These questions may help you to examine your conscience:

Have I been a good friend?

Do I obey my parents?

Have I taken things that belong to other people?

Do I cheat in school or in sports?

Have I told any lies?

Do I take time to pray each day?

Have I used God's name in ways that are not appropriate?

Do I go to church each Sunday?

Am I grateful for the many gifts that God has blessed me with?

The answers to these questions will help you to prepare for the Sacrament of Reconciliation. By taking time to reflect on the questions you will be prepared to speak to the priest when you enter the Reconciliation room.

It's hard for us to remember all the times we have sinned; that's why an examination of conscience is helpful. Sitting in a quiet place and thinking through questions like these will help you to remember times when you have not been the-best-version-of-yourself.

Step 2: We Confess Our Sins

Daniel really loved cookies. One afternoon, he came home from school and his mom was baking a fresh batch of his favorite kind, chocolate chip. The whole house smelled delicious! As he walked into the kitchen his mom said, "Daniel, I know these are your favorite cookies, but I am baking this batch for the church picnic. So, you may only have one." As his mother's back was turned, Daniel quickly grabbed two cookies and ran to his room.

He gobbled down the cookies. They tasted yummy in his mouth, but they left him feeling yucky inside. He knew he had done the wrong thing. Even though he hadn't been caught, he felt terrible.

Daniel was embarrassed, but his conscience encouraged him to go and tell his mother what he had done and to say sorry. His mother gave him a big hug and said, "I am disappointed in you for doing something you knew was wrong, and as a punishment tonight you cannot watch your favorite TV show. But Daniel, I also want you to know that I am very proud of you for saying sorry and admitting that you did the wrong thing. That took a lot of courage."

When the kids in Daniel's class were preparing for their First Reconciliation they asked themselves lots of questions during the examination of conscience. He remembered when he took the extra cookie. He knew it was good that he had apologized to his mom, but he also needed to say sorry to God for stealing. He realized this was something he could confess during Reconciliation.

When you enter the Reconciliation room or confessional, you will sit in a chair across from the priest. After you make the Sign of the Cross it is time for you to confess your sins. You tell the priest about your sins. Remember Daniel from our story? This is when he would talk to the priest about the time he stole the cookie. If you get stuck or nervous, remember, the priest is there to help you.

By talking with the priest about the times that we made poor choices and the times we were not the-best-version-of-ourselves, we rediscover the person God created us to be.

The priest may make some suggestions about how you can grow and become a better person. Remember, although you are sitting with the priest, he is there to represent God. So you are really telling God.

It is also possible to receive this Sacrament behind a screen. The priest sits on the other side of the screen and listens to you as you kneel and confess your sins.

Great champions listen to their coaches so they can get better. Reconciliation is a type of spiritual coaching. Confessing our sins to God is a beautiful way to grow spiritually.

Step 3: We Perform Our Penance

If you ate two dozen donuts every day for a few months, you would become quite sick. While you were eating all those donuts you probably knew that they were not good for you, but you kept eating them anyway.

Then one day you woke up and you came to your senses. You realized that eating all those donuts was making you sick. It's good to be sorry, but it is equally important to change the way we live.

If you had been eating all those donuts and your body was sick, you would need to exercise and eat plenty of fruits and vegetables so your body could get healthy again.

Sin makes our soul sick like bad food makes our body sick. When we go to Reconciliation we say sorry for offending God and making our soul sick, but we also promise to try to live differently in the future.

Before we recite our Act of Contrition, the priest will give us a penance. Penance is a prayer or kind deed that we do to show God that we are really sorry. It is like exercise for the soul to help it get healthy again.

Step 4: We Say Sorry to God

Rachel was angry with her sister. Each time she sat down to do her homework, her sister would bother her, and today Rachel lost her temper and pushed her away. Her sister fell down and started to cry. She had just wanted Rachel to play with her. Rachel felt bad about her choice and apologized to her sister. To show her sister she was really sorry, Rachel said that after she finished her homework she would play any game her sister chose.

After you confess your sins in the Sacrament of Reconciliation, you will pray a prayer of contrition. What is contrition? Contrition means to be sorry. When you pray the words in the prayer of contrition, you are telling God that you are truly sorry for the sins that you have committed.

Here are two examples of an Act of Contrition:

> Dear God, I am sorry for all my sins. I am sorry for the wrong things I have done. I am sorry for the good things I have failed to do. I will do better with your help. Amen.

> My God, I am sorry for my sins with all my heart. In choosing to do wrong and failing to do good, I have sinned against you whom I should love above all things. I firmly intend, with your help, to do penance, to sin no more, and to avoid whatever leads me to sin. Our Savior Jesus Christ suffered and died for us. In his name, my God, have mercy.

> Amen.

Step 5:
The Priest Offers Us Absolution

After the Last Supper, Jesus knew he was going to suffer and die, but he also knew why. He was doing it for you and me, so we could be free from our sins.

Sin makes us unhappy and feels heavy. Jesus didn't want us to feel this way. He wanted us to be free from sin. He wanted us to be able to go to Reconciliation and have our sins forgiven.

After you recite the Act of Contrition the priest will stretch his hands over your head to pray this prayer of absolution:

> **God, the Father of Mercies, through the death and resurrection of his Son, has reconciled the world to himself and sent the Holy Spirit among us for the forgiveness of sins; through the ministry of the Church may God give you pardon and peace, and I absolve you from your sins in the name of the Father, and of the Son, and of the Holy Spirit.**

You will respond: **Amen**.

At the moment of absolution, as the priest extends his hands over you, Jesus is pouring his grace upon you. This is like a bucket of love pouring down upon your head and filling your heart with peace and joy. God's grace also empowers you to make better choices.

After the priest has absolved you of your sins, he will send you forth to walk with God more closely, make better choices, and become the-best-version-of-yourself.

From the Bible: The Prodigal Son

Once upon a time there was a man who had two sons. The younger son came to his father one day and said, "Father, give me the share of your money that will belong to me." The father agreed and a few days later his younger son left and travelled to a distant land, where he wasted all the money on frivolous things.

Soon he had no money and was hungry, so he took a job feeding pigs. He was so hungry he wanted to eat the pigs' food.

One day he was feeding the pigs and he thought to himself, "My father's servants have plenty of food to eat and I am starving. I will go back home, beg my father to forgive me, and ask him to take me back, not as a son but as his servant."

The next day he set off and went to his father. When he was still a far way from home, his father saw him on the horizon. The father was filled with joy and he ran to greet his son, wrapping his arms around him and kissing him.

The son said to his father, "Father, I have sinned against heaven and against you. I am no longer worthy to be called your son. Take me back as a servant." But the father said to his servants, "Quickly, bring out a robe—the best one—and put it on him; put a ring on his finger and sandals on his feet. And get the fatted calf and prepare it so that we can eat and have a great celebration. For this son of mine was lost but now he is found; he was dead, but now he is alive."

Adapted from Luke 15:11—32

Jesus loved to teach in parables because each person in the story teaches us a lesson. In this parable, the father is God the Father. He always rejoices when we return to him. He is not angry with his son; he is delighted that the boy has come home.

There may be times in your life when you feel far from God. But never think that God does not want you to return home. Never think that your sins are greater than God's love.

The son in this story is called the Prodigal Son. Prodigal means "careless and foolish." We are all careless and foolish at times. When we sin we are being careless and foolish. But when we come to Reconciliation we are like the son returning home to his father, and his father rejoices.

First, but Not Last

Reconciliation is a great blessing. You are blessed.

This is your First Reconciliation, but not your last. It is a good idea to get comfortable with the process. It is natural and normal to be nervous, especially the first time. But if you go regularly you will become more comfortable.

Regular Reconciliation is one of the best ways God shares his grace with us. Many of the saints went every month, some even more often.

Going to Reconciliation regularly reminds us of how important it is to focus on growing spiritually and not just physically.

To become the-best-version-of-yourself, grow in virtue, and live a holy life is a lifelong process. Daily prayer, Sunday Mass, and regular Reconciliation are three ways that guide and encourage us in that journey.

Your Best Friend

Friendship is beautiful, but it is also fragile. Sometimes a friend may do things that upset us. This weakens our friendship with him or her. But when that friend says sorry, our friendship is repaired and even strengthened.

God is the best friend you will ever have. Sometimes we do things that offend him. This weakens our friendship with him. We come to the Sacrament of Reconciliation to say sorry to God.

There may be times when you wander away from God. But God will never stop calling to you. He will never stop searching for you. God will never stop encouraging you to become the-best-version-of-yourself, grow in virtue, and live a holy life.

Show What You Know

True or False

1. _____ Ordinary moments can never be great.

2. _____ Your First Reconciliation is one of the great moments in your life.

3. _____ It is never good to prepare for the important moments in your life.

4. _____ God wants us to be restless and unhappy.

5. _____ God's love is greater than any sin you could ever commit.

Fill in the blank

1. God is the best _____ you will ever have.

2. Following your conscience makes you _____ and ignoring your conscience makes you _____.

3. You _____ your sins to the priest.

4. Penance is like _____ for the soul to help it get healthy again.

5. Our Savior _____ suffered and died for us.

6. _____ is essential for a great experience.

7. Confessing your sins through a priest to _____ is a beautiful way to grow spiritually.

8. God's _____ empowers you to make better choices in life.

9. God blesses you with a _____ to help you become the-best-version-of-yourself and live a holy life.

10. God will never stop _____ you to become the-best-version-of-yourself, grow in virtue, and live a holy life.

Word Bank

ENCOURAGING   CONFESS   HAPPY   PREPARATION   UNHAPPY

GRACE   CONSCIENCE   EXERCISE   JESUS   GOD   FRIEND

Journal with Jesus

Dear Jesus,

When I think of you on the cross I am thankful because . . .

_____

_____

_____

_____

_____

_____

_____

_____

_____

Closing Prayer

One of the reasons God invites us to come to Reconciliation is so that we can continue to grow in virtue and happiness, so we can help him build his kingdom. God's kingdom is one of peace, love, and joy. He wants us to share this peace, love, and joy with everyone we meet.

But sometimes rather than humbly helping God build his kingdom, we become selfish and filled with pride and decide to build our own kingdom instead. Can you think of someone in history who focused on trying to build his or her own kingdom instead of helping God build his kingdom of peace, love, and joy?

To praise God and to remind ourselves that our mission is to help God build his kingdom and not get caught up in building our own selfish kingdoms, we pray a prayer called the Glory Be. It is a short but powerful prayer.

Let's all stand up and hold hands and pray it together:

**Glory be to the Father,
and to the Son,
and to the Holy Spirit.
As it was in the beginning,
is now, and ever shall be,
world without end.**

Amen.

6

It's Only the Beginning

God, our loving Father,
thank you for all the ways you bless me.
Help me to be aware that every person,
place, and adventure I experience is an
opportunity to love you more.
Fill me with a desire to change and to grow,
and give me the grace to become
the-best-version-of-myself in
every moment of every day.

Amen.

So Much to Look Forward To

We are so blessed to have God as our Father. We are so blessed to have Jesus as our friend and Savior. We are so blessed to have the Holy Spirit to lead and guide us.

Remember, God wants you to become the-best-version-of-yourself, grow in virtue, and live a holy life.

He gives us his grace through great moments like Baptism, First Reconciliation, First Communion, and Confirmation. But when we go to Mass on Sunday and spend a few minutes each day praying, he also gives us the grace we need to thrive every day.

The Will of God and Happiness

Prayer also helps us to discover God's will for our lives. It is by doing his will that we become the-best-version-of-ourselves and live holy lives. As we grow in wisdom we also discover that we are happiest when we are trying to do God's will, because it leads to happiness in this life and happiness for eternity with God in heaven.

Is it difficult to know God's will? Sometimes it is. But most of the time we know what God wants us to do.

God wants us to make good choices
and avoid bad choices.

God wants us to do things that are good
and avoid things that are bad.

God wants us to be a good son or daughter,
and God wants us to be a good friend.

For the most part you already know what God's will is. But every day he talks to us all in different ways to help us know his will more clearly.

The Prayer Process

God loves it when we talk to him. He loves it when we talk to him in our hearts throughout the day. He also loves it when we take a few minutes each day just to talk to him.

We call this conversation with God prayer. Sometimes when we sit down to pray we don't know what to say to him. The Prayer Process is a simple way to make sure we always have something to say to God. It is made up of seven easy steps. Each step is designed to guide your daily conversation with God.

1. Thank God for whomever and whatever you are most grateful today.

2. Think about yesterday. Talk to God about the times when you were and were not the-best-version-of-yourself.

3. What do you think God is trying to say to you today? Talk to him about that.

4. Ask God to forgive you for anything you have done wrong and to fill your heart with peace.

5. Talk to God about some way he is inviting you to change and grow.

6. Pray for the other people in your life by asking God to guide them and watch over them.

7. Pray the Our Father.

This is a simple way to have a conversation with God each day during your quiet time. Through prayer God helps us to become the-best-version-of-ourselves, grow in virtue, and live holy lives.

The Power of Great Habits

Habits play a very important role in our lives. There are good habits and bad habits. Good habits help us become the-best-version-of-ourselves. Bad habits stop us from becoming all God created us to be.

Your parents, teachers, and coaches are all working very hard to help you develop good habits. Here are some examples of good habits:

- Drinking lots of water

- Eating fruits and vegetables

- Reading every day

- Spending time with friends

- Encouraging the people around you

- Going to church on Sunday

- Praying for a few minutes every day

Here are some examples of bad habits:

- Watching too much TV

- Eating too much junk food

- Not taking care of your things

- Bullying other children

- Missing Mass on Sunday

Daily Prayer

The champions of every sport become great champions by having great habits. They practice hard and eat healthy foods. The champions of our faith became saints by having great habits. They practiced being patient and kind, generous and compassionate—and they prayed every day.

The habit of daily prayer will help you discover the voice of God in your life and give you the courage to do what God is inviting you to do.

The Prayer Process is a great habit that will help you to become the-best-version-of-yourself and live a holy life.

We find incredible happiness in doing God's will. By spending a few minutes in quiet prayer each day and going to Mass each Sunday you will discover God's will for your life.

You are blessed. The more you embrace the habit of daily prayer, the more blessed you will become.

From the Bible:
Jesus Went to a Quiet Place

One day Jesus was having dinner at a friend's house. When the people in the village heard that Jesus was there, they brought their sick friends and relatives to him and asked him to heal them. He healed the sick and the people were amazed. Very early the next morning Jesus went off alone and found a quiet place so he could pray.

This is only one of many times in the Bible when we read about Jesus going off to a quiet place to pray. We all need a few minutes each day in a quiet place to sit and talk with God.

One of the best habits you can develop in life is the habit of daily prayer.

Sometimes when you sit down to spend some quiet time with God in prayer you don't know what to say. So, to help you with that, we have taught you the Prayer Process to guide your daily conversation with God.

If Jesus needed quiet time, don't you think we do too?

Be Grateful

The best way to begin each day is by being grateful. Thanking God for another day is a simple way to talk to him as we get out of bed each morning.

Being grateful is also the best way to begin our daily prayer—that's why the first step in the Prayer Process is about GRATITUDE.

By taking time to reflect on all the ways God has blessed us we become filled with gratitude and God fills us with joy. So anytime you are sad or feeling a little down, talk to God about everyone and everything you are grateful for.

It might help to make a gratitude list. Some people make a gratitude list and carry it around with them everywhere they go, in their pocket, wallet, or purse. Then if something bad happens or they are feeling a little down, they take out their gratitude list and pray through it.

Let's make our very own gratitude list together now.

I am grateful for . . .

_____

_____

_____

_____

_____

_____

_____

_____

God Fills You With Joy

Throughout your life there are going to be many wonderful things that happen. There are also going to be days when things happen that get you down a bit. Whether you are having a great day or a not-so-good day, it's always a good idea to spend a few minutes talking to God about all you are grateful for. We praise God by being grateful, and he responds by filling us with joy.

Congratulations!

Congratulations on making your First Reconciliation. This is a wonderful time in your life. You are blessed.

The next great Catholic Moment in your journey will be your First Communion.

We hope the lessons you have learned in preparing for your First Reconciliation will live in your heart forever. We hope they will help you become the-best-version-of-yourself, grow in virtue, and live a holy life. We hope they will help you to never forget that YOU ARE BLESSED!

Show What You Know

True or False

1. _____ You are blessed to have God as your Father.

2. _____ Prayer helps you discover God's will for your life.

3. _____ Jesus always went to a loud place to speak with God.

4. _____ God wants to tell you something every time you go to Mass.

5. _____ Gratitude fills us with joy.

Fill in the blank

1. Doing God's will leads to happiness in this life

   and _____ for eternity with God in heaven.

2. God wants to _____ you in a thousand different ways so you can live a fabulous life.

3. It is by doing God's will that you become

   _____.

4. The more you embrace the habit of daily _____ the more blessed you will become.

5. As you grow in _____ you will discover that you are happiest when you are trying to do God's will.

6. God wants us to do things that are _____ and avoid _____ choices.

7. Jesus is your _____ and _____.

8. One great way to have a daily conversation with God is by using the _____ _____.

9. The champions of our Catholic faith become saints by having great _____.

10. The best way to begin each day is by being _____.

Word Bank

BLESS   GOOD   BAD   HABITS   WISDOM   SAVIOR   PRAYER   FRIEND

THE-BEST-VERSION-OF-YOURSELF   PRAYER PROCESS   HAPPINESS   GRATEFUL

Journal with Jesus

Dear Jesus,

I am so blessed to have had my First Reconciliation because . . .

_____

_____

_____

_____

_____

_____

_____

Closing Prayer

Saint Francis of Assisi lived in Italy about 800 years ago. He loved God very much and dedicated his life to teaching people about Jesus. This beautiful prayer of St. Francis was written to help us put things in perspective. It is so easy to get confused about what matters most. Prayer helps us get our priorities straight. Let's pray Saint Francis' prayer together:

Lord, make me an instrument of your peace:
where there is hatred, let me sow love;
where there is injury, pardon;
where there is doubt, faith;
where there is despair, hope;
where there is darkness, light;
where there is sadness, joy.

O Divine Master, grant that I may not so much seek
to be consoled as to console,
to be understood as to understand,
to be loved as to love.
For it is in giving that we receive,
it is in pardoning that we are pardoned,
and it is in dying that we are born to eternal life.

Amen.

My Little Catechism

Your fabulous journey with God is just beginning. Along the way you will have many questions. Questions are good. God places questions in your heart and mind for many different reasons. Follow your questions, wherever they might lead you.

Some of your questions will be easy to find answers to. To help us answer many of our questions, our spiritual leaders have given us the Catechism of the Catholic Church. The answers we find there have been revealed by God and by nature over the centuries.

In the pages that follow we will share with you some questions you may have about God and life. The answers are easy to read but often hard to live. But the answers will help you become the-best-version-of-yourself, grow in virtue, and live a holy life.

There will be other times in your life when you have questions that cannot be answered by words on a page, such as what Vocation you are called to or what career you should pursue. At these times you will seek deeply personal answers to deeply personal questions.

These questions require a lot more patience. Seek the advice of wise people who love the Lord. Read what wise men and women before you have had to say on such topics. But, most of all, pray and ask God to show you his way.

As you make this journey you will encounter others who have questions. Help them as best you can to find the answers. People deserve answers to their questions.

And never, ever, forget . . . you are blessed!

1. **Q: Who made you?**

   A: God made you.

   > In the Bible: Genesis 1:1, 26–27; Genesis 2:7, 21–22
   > In the *Catechism*: CCC, 355

2. **Q: Does God love you?**

   A: Yes. God loves you more than anyone in the world,
   and more than you could ever imagine.

   > In the Bible: John 3:16
   > In the *Catechism*: CCC, 457, 458

3. **Q: Why did God make you?**

   A: God made you to know him, love him, to carry out the mission he entrusts to
   you in this world, and to be happy with him forever in Heaven.

   > In the Bible: Deuteronomy 10:12–15; John 17:3
   > In the *Catechism*: CCC, 1, 358

4. **Q: What is God?**

   A: God is an infinite and perfect spirit.

   > In the Bible: Exodus 3:6; Isaiah 44:6; 1 John 4:8, 16
   > In the *Catechism*: CCC, 198–200, 212, 221

5. **Q: Did God have a beginning?**

   A: No. God has no beginning. He always was and he always will be.

   > In the Bible: Psalm 90:2; Revelation 1:8
   > In the *Catechism*: CCC, 202

6. **Q: Where is God?**

   A: Everywhere

   > In the Bible: Psalm 139
   > In the *Catechism*: CCC, 1

7. **Q: Does God see us?**

   A: God sees us and watches over us.

   > In the Bible: Wisdom 11:24–26; Jeremiah 1:5
   > In the *Catechism*: CCC, 37, 301, 302

8. **Q: Does God know everything?**

   A: Yes. God knows all things, even our most secret thoughts, words, and actions.

   > In the Bible: Job 21:22; Psalm 33:13–15; Psalm 147:4–5
   > In the *Catechism*: CCC, 208

9. **Q: Is God all loving, just, holy, and merciful?**

   A: Yes, God is loving, all just, all holy, and all merciful—and he invites us to be loving, just, holy, and merciful too.

   > In the Bible: John 13:34; 1 John 4:8; Ephesians 2:4
   > In the *Catechism*: CCC, 214, 211, 208

10. **Q: Is there only one God?**

    A: Yes, there is only one God.

    > In the Bible: Isaiah 44:6; John 8:58
    > In the *Catechism*: CCC, 253

11. **Q: Why is there only one God?**

    A: There can only be one God, because God, being supreme and infinite, cannot have an equal.

    > In the Bible: Mark 12:29–30
    > In the *Catechism*: CCC, 202

12. **Q: How many Persons are there in God?**

    A: In God there are three Divine Persons, unique and distinct and yet equal in all things—the Father, the Son, and the Holy Spirit.

    > In the Bible: 1 Corinthians 12:4–6; 2 Corinthians 13:13; Ephesians 4:4–6
    > In the *Catechism*: CCC, 252, 254, 255

13. **Q: Is the Father God?**

    A: Yes.

    > In the Bible: Exodus 3:6; Exodus 4:22
    > In the *Catechism*: CCC, 253, 262

14. **Q: Is the Son God?**

    A: Yes.

    > In the Bible: John 8:58; John 10:30
    > In the *Catechism*: CCC, 253, 262

15. **Q: Is the Holy Spirit God?**

    A: Yes.

    > In the Bible: John 14:26; John 15:26
    > In the *Catechism*: CCC, 253, 263

16. **Q: What is the Holy Trinity?**

    A: The Holy Trinity is one God in three divine persons—Father, Son, and Holy Spirit.

    > In the Bible: Matthew 28:19
    > In the *Catechism*: CCC, 249, 251

17. **Q. What is free will?**

    A: Free will is an incredible gift from God that allows us to make our own decisions. This incredible gift comes with incredible responsibility.

    > In the Bible: Sirach 15:14—15
    > In the *Catechism*: CCC, 1731

18. **Q. What is sin?**

    A: Sin is any willful thought, word, deed, or omission contrary to the law of God.

    > In the Bible: Genesis 3:5; Exodus 20:1—17
    > In the *Catechism*: CCC, 1850

19. **Q: How many kinds of sin are there?**

    A: There are two actual kinds of sin—venial and mortal.

    > In the Bible: 1 John 5:16—17
    > In the *Catechism*: CCC, 1855

20. **Q: What is a venial sin?**

    A: A venial sin is a slight offense against God.

    > In the Bible: Matthew 5:19; Matthew 12:32; 1 John 5:16—18
    > In the *Catechism*: CCC, 1855, 1863

21. **Q: What is a mortal sin?**

    A: A mortal sin is a grievous offense against God and his law.

    > In the Bible: Matthew 12:32; 1 John 5:16—18
    > In the *Catechism*: CCC, 1855, 1857

22. **Q: Does God abandon us when we sin?**

A: Never. God is always calling to us, pleading with us, to return to him and his ways.

In the Bible: Psalm 103: 9–10, 13; Jeremiah 3:22; Matthew 28:20; Luke 15:11–32
In the *Catechism: CCC,* 27, 55, 982

23. **Q: Which Person of the Holy Trinity became man?**

A: The Second Person, God the Son, became man without giving up his divine nature.

In the Bible: 1 John 4:2
In the *Catechism: CCC,* 423, 464

24. **Q: What name was given to the Second Person of the Holy Trinity when he became man?**

A: Jesus.

In the Bible: Luke 1:31; Matthew 1:21
In the *Catechism: CCC,* 430

25. **Q: When the Son became man, did he have a human mother?**

A: Yes.

In the Bible: Luke 1:26–27
In the *Catechism: CCC,* 488, 490, 495

26. **Q: Who was Jesus' mother?**

A: The Blessed Virgin Mary.

In the Bible: Luke 1:30, 31; Matthew 1:21–23
In the *Catechism: CCC,* 488, 495

27. **Q: Why do we honor Mary?**

A: Because she is the mother of Jesus and our mother too.

In the Bible: Luke 1:48; John 19:27
In the *Catechism: CCC,* 971

28. **Q: Who was Jesus' real father?**

A: God the Father.

In the Bible: Luke 1:35; John 17:1
In the *Catechism: CCC,* 422, 426, 442

29. Q: **Who was Jesus' foster father?**

A: Joseph.

> In the Bible: Matthew 1:19, 20; Matthew 2:13, 19—21
> In the *Catechism*: CCC, 437, 488, 1655

30. Q: **Is Jesus God, or is he man, or is he both God and man?**

A: Jesus is both God and man; as the Second Person of the Holy Trinity, he is God; and since he took on a human nature from his mother Mary, he is man.

> In the Bible: Philippians 2:6—7; John 1:14, 16; John 13:3; 1 John 4:2
> In the *Catechism*: CCC, 464, 469

31. Q: **Was Jesus also a man?**

A: Yes, Jesus was fully God and fully human.

> In the Bible: Luke 24:39; 1 John 4:2—3
> In the *Catechism*: CCC, 464, 469, 470

32. Q: **On what day was Jesus born?**

A: Jesus was born on Christmas day in a stable in Bethlehem.

> In the Bible: Luke 2:1—20; Matthew 1:18—25
> In the *Catechism*: CCC, 437, 563

33. Q: **What is the Incarnation?**

A: The Incarnation is the belief that Jesus became man.

> In the Bible: John 1:14; 1 John 4:2
> In the *Catechism*: CCC, 461, 463

34. Q: **Did Jesus love life?**

A: Yes.

> In the Bible: John 10:10; John 2:1—12
> In the *Catechism*: CCC, 221, 257, 989

35. Q: **If Jesus loved life why did he willingly die on the cross?**

A: He died on the cross because he loved you and me even more than life.

> In the Bible: Romans 5:8; John 15:13; Ephesians 5:2
> In the *Catechism*: CCC, 1825, 604

36. **Q: Why did Jesus suffer and die?**

A: So that we could be forgiven our sins, and live with him in heaven forever after this life.

> In the Bible: John 3:16; 2 Corinthians 5:14–16
> In the *Catechism*: CCC, 604, 618, 620

37. **Q: What do we call the mystery of God becoming man?**

A: The mystery of the Incarnation.

> In the Bible: John 1:14; 1 John 4:2
> In the *Catechism*: CCC, 461, 463

38. **Q: On what day did Jesus die on the cross?**

A: Good Friday, the day after the Last Supper.

> In the Bible: John 19:16–40; Matthew 27:33–50
> In the *Catechism*: CCC, 641

39. **Q: On what day did Jesus rise from the dead?**

A: On Easter Sunday, three days after Good Friday.

> In the Bible: Matthew 28:1–6; Mark 16:1–8
> In the *Catechism*: CCC, 1169, 1170

40. **Q: What gifts do we receive as a result of being saved by Jesus?**

A: By dying on the cross Jesus restored our relationship with God and opened a floodgate of grace.

> In the Bible: Luke 23:44–46; Romans 3:21–26; 2 Corinthians 5:17–21
> In the *Catechism*: CCC, 1026, 1047

41. **Q: What is grace?**

A: Grace is the help God gives us to respond generously to his call, to do what is good and right, grow in virtue, and live holy lives.

> In the Bible: John 1:12–18; 2 Corinthians 12:9
> In the *Catechism*: CCC, 1996

42. **Q: What is Faith?**

A: Faith is a gift from God. It is a supernatural virtue that allows us to firmly believe all the truth that God has revealed to us.

> In the Bible: Hebrews 11:1
> In the *Catechism*: CCC, 1814

43. **Q: What is Hope?**

A: Hope is a gift from God. It is a supernatural virtue that allows us to firmly trust that God will keep all his promises and lead us to heaven.

In the Bible: Romans 8:24–25; 1 Timothy 4:10; 1 Timothy 1:1; Hebrews 6:18–20
In the Catechism: CCC, 1817, 1820–1821

44. **Q: What is Charity?**

A: Charity is a gift from God. It is a supernatural virtue that allows us to love God above everything else, and our neighbor as ourselves.

In the Bible: John 13:34; 1 Corinthians 13:4–13
In the Catechism: CCC, 1822, 1823, 1825

45. **Q: Will God give you the gifts of Faith, Hope, and Charity?**

A: Yes, God gives the gifts of Faith, Hope, and Charity, freely to all those who ask for them sincerely and consistently.

In the Bible: 1 Corinthians 13:13
In the Catechism: 1813

46. **Q: How long will God love me for?**

A: God will love you forever.

In the Bible: John 13:1; Romans 8:35–39
In the Catechism: CCC, 219

47. **Q: When did Jesus ascend into heaven?**

A: On Ascension Thursday, forty days after Easter.

In the Bible: Acts 1:9; Mark 16:19
In the Catechism: CCC, 659

48. **Q: When did the Holy Spirit descend upon the Apostles?**

A: On Pentecost Sunday, fifty days after Easter.

In the Bible: John 20:21–22; Matthew 28:19
In the Catechism: CCC, 731, 1302

49. **Q: What is meant by the Redemption?**

A: Redemption means that Jesus' Incarnation, life, death, and Resurrection paid the price for our sins, opened the gates of heaven, and freed us from slavery to sin and death.

In the Bible: Ephesians 1:7; Romans 4:25
In the Catechism: CCC, 517, 606, 613

50. **Q: What did Jesus establish to continue his mission of Redemption?**

A: He established the Catholic Church.

In the Bible: Matthew 16:18
In the Catechism: CCC, 773, 778, 817, 822

51. **Q: Why do we believe that the Catholic Church is the one true Church?**

A: Because it is the only Church established by Jesus.

In the Bible: Matthew 16:18
In the Catechism: CCC, 750

52. **Q: Does it matter to which Church or religion you belong?**

A: Yes, in order to be faithful to Jesus, it is necessary to remain in the Church he established.

In the Bible: Mark 16:16; John 3:5
In the Catechism: CCC, 846

53. **Q: What are the Four Marks of the Church?**

A: One, Holy, Catholic, and Apostolic.

In the Bible: Ephesians 2:20, 4:3, 5:26; Matthew 28:19; Revelation 21:14;
In the Catechism: CCC, 813, 823, 830, 857

54. **Q: How does the Church preserve the teachings of Jesus?**

A: Through Sacred Scripture and Sacred Tradition.

In the Bible: 2 Timothy 2:2; 2 Thessalonians 2:15
In the Catechism: CCC, 78, 81, 82

55. **Q: How does the Church's calendar differ from the secular calendar?**

A: The first day of the Church's year is the first Sunday of Advent, not January 1. The Church's calendar revolves around the life, death, and Resurrection of Jesus. Throughout the course of the Church's year the whole mystery of Jesus Christ is unfolded.

In the Bible: Luke 2:1–20; 1 Corinthians 15:3–4
In the Catechism: CCC, 1163; 1171, 1194

Going Deeper

Over the course of the year, through the readings at Mass, the feast days and holy days, we experience the story of Jesus. The Church's calendar does this to remind us that Jesus' story is not just about what happened over two thousand years ago. It is about our friendship with him today. The mystery of his life, teachings, and saving grace is unfolding in your life and the life of the Church today.

56. Q: **Did Jesus give special authority to one of the Apostles?**
    A: Yes, to Peter when Jesus said to him, "I will give you the keys of the kingdom of heaven, and whatever you bind on earth shall be bound in heaven, and whatever you loose on earth shall be loosed in heaven."

    In the Bible: Mark 3:16, 9:2; Luke 24:34
    In the *Catechism*: CCC, 552, 881

57. Q: **Who speaks with the authority that Jesus gave to St. Peter?**
    A: The pope who is St. Peter's successor, the Bishop of Rome, and the Vicar of Christ on earth.

    In the Bible: Matthew 16:18; John 21:15–17
    In the *Catechism*: CCC, 891

58. Q: **What is the name of the present pope?**
    A: Pope Francis.

    In the Bible: Matthew 16:18; John 21:15–17
    In the *Catechism*: CCC, 936

59. Q: **What is the sacred liturgy?**
    A: The Church's public worship of God.

    In the Bible: John 4:23–24
    In the *Catechism*: CCC, 1069, 1070

60. Q: **What attitude should we have when we participate in the sacred liturgy?**
    A: We should have the attitude of reverence in our hearts and respect in our actions and appearance.

    In the Bible: Hebrews 12:28
    In the *Catechism*: CCC, 2097

61. **Q: What is a Sacrament?**

   A: A Sacrament is an outward sign, instituted by Christ and entrusted to the Church to give grace. Grace bears fruit in those who receive them with the required dispositions.

   In the Bible: 2 Peter 1:4
   In the *Catechism*: CCC, 1131

   Going Deeper

   God gives you grace to help you do what is good and right. When you are open to God, he also gives you the grace to be kind, generous, courageous, and compassionate toward others. Grace bears good fruit in our lives. One of the most powerful ways God shares his grace with us is through the Sacraments. This grace helps us to become the-very-best-version-of-ourselves, grow in virtue, and live holy lives.

62. **Q: How does Jesus share his life with us?**

   A: During his earthly life, Jesus shared his life with others through his words and actions; now he shares the very same life with us through the Sacraments.

   In the Bible: John 3:16; John 6:5–7
   In the *Catechism*: CCC, 521; 1131, 1115–1116

   Going Deeper

   God loves to share his life and love with us. We can experience his life through daily prayer, Scripture, and through serving one another. The most powerful way that God shares his life with us is through the Sacraments. Sunday Mass and regular Reconciliation are two Sacraments that guide us and encourage us on our journey to become the-best-version-of-ourselves, grow in virtue, and live holy lives.

63. **Q: How many Sacraments are there?**

   A: Seven.

   In the Bible: John 20:22–23; Luke 22:14–20; John 7:37–39; James 5:14–16; Hebrews 5:1–6; Matthew 19:6
   In the *Catechism*: CCC, 1113

64. **Q: What are the Seven Sacraments; and which ones have you received?**

   A: Baptism, Penance, Holy Eucharist, Confirmation, Holy Orders, Matrimony, Anointing of the Sick. You have received Baptism, Penance, and Holy Eucharist.

   In the Bible: John 20:22–23; Luke 22:14–20; John 7:37–39; James 5:14–16; Hebrews 5:1–6; Matthew 19:6
   In the *Catechism*: CCC, 1113

65. **Q: What are the Sacraments you can only receive once?**

A: Baptism, Confirmation, and Holy Orders.

In the Bible: Ephesians 4:30
In the *Catechism: CCC,* 1272

66. **Q: How is Christian initiation accomplished?**

A: Christian initiation is accomplished with three Sacraments: Baptism which is the beginning of new life; Confirmation which strengthens our new life in Christ; and the Eucharist which nourishes the disciple with Jesus' Body and Blood so that we can be transformed in Christ.

In the Bible: John 3:5; Acts 8:14–17; John 6:51–58
In the *Catechism: CCC,* 1212; 1275

Going Deeper

Life is a journey with God. Baptism, Confirmation and First Communion are all great moments in your journey. They are Sacraments that work together to help you live your best life. In Baptism you receive new life in Jesus, in Confirmation God reminds us that he has a special mission for each and every single one of us, and Holy Communion gives us the strength and the wisdom to live that mission by serving God and others.

67. **Q: When you were born, did you have Sanctifying Grace (a share in God's life)?**

A: No.

In the Bible: Colossians 1:12–14
In the *Catechism: CCC,* 403, 1250

68. **Q: Why are we not born with Sanctifying Grace?**

A: Because we are born with original sin, which is the loss of Sanctifying Grace.

In the Bible: Genesis 3:23
In the *Catechism: CCC,* 403, 1250

69. **Q: Was any human person conceived without original sin?**

A: Yes, Mary at her Immaculate Conception.

In the Bible: Luke 1:28
In the *Catechism: CCC,* 491, 492

70. Q: What was the original sin?

A: Adam and Eve were tempted by the devil, and they chose to distrust God's goodness and to disobey his law.

In the Bible: Genesis 3:1–11; Romans 5:19
In the Catechism: CCC, 397

71. Q: Is there really a devil?

A: Yes.

In the Bible: 1 John 5:19; 1 Peter 5:8
In the Catechism: CCC, 391

72. Q: Is it easier to be bad or to be good?

A: It is easier to be bad, because original sin has left us with an inclination to sin called concupiscence.

In the Bible: Romans 7:15–18
In the Catechism: CCC, 409, 12z, 2516

73. Q: When did you receive Sanctifying Grace for the first time?

A: At Baptism.

In the Bible: 2 Corinthians 5:17
In the Catechism: CCC, 1265

74. Q: What is Baptism?

A: Baptism is the Sacrament of rebirth in Jesus that is necessary for salvation.

In the Bible: 2 Corinthians 5:17; 2 Peter 1:4; Galatians 4:5–7
In the Catechism: CCC, 1266, 1277, 1279

Going Deeper

Baptism is a great blessing. Through your Baptism you became a member of the Catholic Church. This is another wonderful reason why being Catholic is a great blessing. Through your Baptism, you received new life in Jesus. You were made for mission. God had that mission in mind when you were baptized, and every day since he has been preparing you for your mission. We discover that mission through prayer, the Sacraments, and service to others. God doesn't reveal our mission all at once, he reveals it step-by-step.

75. **Q: What are the fruits of Baptism?**

A: Baptism makes us Christians, cleanses us of original sin and personal sin, and reminds us that we are children of God and members of the Body of Christ—the Church.

In the Bible: Galatians 4:5–7
In the Catechism: CCC, 1279

Going Deeper

In Baptism God gives us many gifts. We become Christian, our sins are forgiven, we are given new life in Jesus, and God marks us for a great mission. God is able to do this through the power of the Holy Spirit. In Baptism our souls are flooded with the gift of the Holy Spirit, which helps us in our journey to grow closer to God. Each and every Sacrament we receive is full of gifts, big and small. Every blessing reminds us that we are all sons and daughters of a loving Father.

76. **Q: What did Baptism do for you?**

A: It gave me a share in God's life for the first time, made me a child of God, and took away original sin.

In the Bible: 2 Corinthians 5:17; 2 Peter 1:4; Galatians 4:5–7
In the Catechism: CCC, 1266, 1279

77. **Q: How old does someone need to be to receive Baptism?**

A: A person can be baptized at any age. Since the earliest times of Christianity, Baptism has been administered to infant children because Baptism is a grace and a gift that is freely given by God and does not presuppose any human merit.

In the Bible: Acts 2:37–39
In the Catechism: CCC, 1282

Going Deeper

God's love is a free gift. There is nothing you could do to earn or lose God's love. You may be tempted to think that God's love is something to be earned. This is simply not true. God loved you into life, and God loved you into the Church. You did nothing to be born, and if you were baptized as an infant you did nothing to be baptized. You didn't do anything to deserve life or Baptism. God freely gives you life and faith.

78. **Q: Who administers the Sacrament of Baptism?**

A: Anyone can administer the Sacrament of Baptism in an emergency by pouring water over that person's head and saying, "I baptize you in the name of the Father, and of the Son, and of the Holy Spirit." Baptism, however, is usually administered by a priest or deacon.

In the Bible: Matthew 28:19
In the *Catechism*: CCC, 1284

Going Deeper

Not everyone is baptized as an infant. Some people don't learn about Jesus until they are adults. But God wants everyone to receive the blessing of Baptism. He wants everyone to be a part of his family—the Catholic Church. He wants everyone to be free from original sin. He wants everyone to have new life in his Son Jesus. He wants everyone to spend eternity with him in heaven.

79. **Q: How long do you remain a child of God?**

A: Forever.

In the Bible: 1 Peter 1:3—4
In the *Catechism*: CCC, 1272, 1274

80. **Q: Can you lose a share in God's life after Baptism?**

A: Yes.

In the Bible: Mark 3:29
In the *Catechism*: CCC, 1861

81. **Q: Can we lose the new life of grace that God has freely given us?**

A: Yes. The new life of grace can be lost by sin.

In the Bible: 1 Corinthians 6:9; 2 Corinthians 5:19—21; 1 John 1:9
In the *Catechism*: CCC, 1420

Going Deeper

At Baptism we are filled with a very special grace. This grace blesses us with new life and brings us into friendship with God. That new life can be hurt or lost when we sin. When that happens, don't worry because God has given us the blessing of Reconciliation! As long as we are truly sorry for our sins and go to Reconciliation, we can once again experience the fullness of life with God. Reconciliation is a great blessing!

82. **Q: How can you lose Sanctifying Grace (a share in God's life)?**

A: By committing mortal sin.

> In the Bible: Galatians 5:19–21; Romans 1:28–32
> In the *Catechism*: CCC, 1861

83. **Q: Which is the worse sin: venial or mortal?**

A: Mortal (deadly) sin.

> In the Bible: 1 John 5:16
> In the *Catechism*: CCC, 1855, 1874, 1875

84. **Q: What three things are necessary to commit a mortal sin?**

A: 1. You must disobey God in a serious matter.

2. You must know that it is wrong.

3. You must freely choose to do it anyway.

> In the Bible: Mark 10:19; Luke 16:19–31; James 2:10–11
> In the *Catechism*: CCC, 1857

85. **Q: What happens to you if you die in a state of mortal sin?**

A: You go to hell.

> In the Bible: 1 John 3:14–15; Matthew 25:41–46
> In the *Catechism*: CCC, 1035, 1472, 1861, 1874

86. **Q: Is there really a hell?**

A: Yes; it is the place of eternal separation from God.

> In the Bible: Isaiah 66:24; Mark 9:47, 48
> In the *Catechism*: CCC, 1035

87. **Q: What happens if you die with venial sin on your soul?**

A: You go to purgatory where you are purified and made perfect.

> In the Bible: 1 Corinthians 3:14–15; 2 Maccabees 12:45–46
> In the *Catechism*: CCC, 1030, 1031, 1472

88. **Q: What happens to the souls in purgatory after their purification?**

A: They go to heaven.

> In the Bible: 2 Maccabees 12:45
> In the *Catechism*: CCC, 1030

89. **Q: Is there really a heaven?**

A: Yes; it is the place of eternal happiness with God.

> In the Bible: 1 John 3:2; 1 Corinthians 13:12; Revelation 22:4–5
> In the Catechism: CCC, 1023, 1024

90. **Q: Can any sin, no matter how serious, be forgiven?**

A: Yes, any sin, no matter how serious or how many times it is committed, can be forgiven.

> In the Bible: Matthew 18:21–22
> In the Catechism: CCC, 982

91. **Q: What is the primary purpose of the Sacrament of Reconciliation?**

A: The primary purpose of the Sacrament of Reconciliation is the forgiveness of sins committed after Baptism.

> In the Bible: Sirach 18:12–13; Sirach 21:1; Acts 26:17–18
> In the Catechism: CCC, 1421, 1446, 1468

Going Deeper

Through Baptism we become children of God, are welcomed into a life of grace, and given the promise of heaven. As we get older, we may do things that harm our relationship with God. But God keeps loving us, and invites us to participate in regular Reconciliation so that our friendship with him can always be as strong as it was in Baptism. If we offend God, the best thing to do is to say sorry to God by going to Reconciliation.

92. **Q: What other names is the Sacrament of Reconciliation known by?**

A: In different places and different times, the Sacrament of Reconciliation is also called the Sacrament of Conversion, Confession, or Penance.

> In the Bible: Mark 1:15; Proverbs 28:13; Acts 3:19; 2 Peter 3:9
> In the Catechism: CCC, 1423, 1424

Going Deeper

Jesus loves you and he wants to save you from your sins. He wants to save you because he wants to live in friendship with you on earth and in heaven. He wants to share his joy with you and he wants you to share that joy with others. No matter what name is used, the Sacrament of Reconciliation restores our friendship with God and helps us become the-best-version-of-ourselves, grow in virtue, and live a holy life.

93. Q: **Is the Sacrament of Reconciliation a blessing?**

A: Yes, it is a great blessing from God.

In the Bible: Psalm 32:1–2; Romans 4:6–8
In the Catechism: CCC, 1468, 1496

94. Q: **Who commits sins?**

A: All people sin.

In the Bible: Romans 3:23–25; 1 John 1:8–10
In the Catechism: CCC, 827

95. Q: **How can a mortal sin be forgiven?**

A: Through the Sacrament of Reconciliation.

In the Bible: 2 Corinthians 5:20–21
In the Catechism: CCC, 1446, 1497

96. Q: **What is the ordinary way for someone to be reconciled with God and his Church?**

A: The ordinary way for someone to be reconciled with God and his Church is by personally confessing all grave sin to a priest, followed by receiving absolution.

In the Bible: John 20:23
In the Catechism: CCC, 1497

Going Deeper

We all stray away from God from time to time. When we do, it is a good time to go to the Sacrament of Reconciliation and say sorry to God. You might be tempted to fall into the trap of thinking that your sin is too big for God to forgive. But, there is nothing you can do that will make God stop loving you. The doors of the Church are always open and God is always willing to forgive us when we are sorry. The Sacrament of Reconciliation is a great blessing!

97. Q: **What three things must you do in order to receive forgiveness of sin in the Sacrament of Confession?**

A: 1. You must be truly sorry for your sins.
   2. Confess all mortal sins in kind and number committed since your last Confession.
   3. You must resolve to amend your life.

In the Bible: Romans 8:17; Romans 3:23–26
In the Catechism: CCC, 1448

Going Deeper

When we sin we become restless and unhappy. God doesn't want us to be restless and unhappy so he invites us to come to Reconciliation so that he can fill us with his joy. There may be times in your life when you feel far from God. But never think that God doesn't want you to return to him. Never think that your sins are greater than God's love. God's love and mercy will always be waiting for you in the Sacrament of Reconciliation.

98. **Q: What are the three actions required of us in the Sacrament of Reconciliation?**

A: The three actions required of us in the Sacrament of Reconciliation are repentance, confession of sins to the priest, and the intention to atone for our sins by performing the penance given by the priest.

In the Bible: 1 John 1:9
In the Catechism: CCC, 1491

Going Deeper

Regular Reconciliation is one of the most powerful ways that God shares his grace and mercy with us. God asks us to be sorry for our sins, confess them out loud to a priest, and do an act of penance so that our friendship with God can be restored and strengthened. The more you go to Reconciliation the more you will come to realize the incredible power of God's grace and mercy in your life.

99. **Q: Who has the power to forgive sin?**

A: Jesus Christ through a Catholic priest.

In the Bible: John 20:23; 2 Corinthians 5:18
In the Catechism: CCC, 1461, 1493, 1495

100. **Q: Can the priest talk about your sins with other people?**

A: No. The priest must keep secret all sins confessed to him.

In the Bible: 2 Corinthians 5:18–19
In the Catechism: CCC, 1467

Going Deeper

If you are nervous about going to Confession, it's OK. Being nervous is natural. Just know that the priest is there to help you. He will not think poorly of you because of your sins or tell anyone what they are. Instead, he will be happy that you went to Confession. Remember, the priest is there to encourage you, extend God's love and mercy to you, and to help you grow in virtue.

101. **Q: What is the purpose of penance?**

A: After you have confessed your sins, the priest will propose penance for you to perform. The purpose of these acts of penance is to repair the harm caused by sin and to re-establish the habits of a disciple of Christ.

In the Bible: Luke 19:8; Acts 2:38
In the Catechism: CCC, 1459–1460

Going Deeper

Friendship is beautiful but it is also fragile. God gives us the Sacrament of Reconciliation to heal the pain caused by sin and to repair our friendship with him. When we do our penance we show God that we are truly sorry. Penance helps our souls get healthy again.

102. **Q: How often should you go to Confession?**

A: You should go immediately if you are in a state of mortal sin; otherwise, it is recommended to go once a month because it is highly recommended to confess venial sins. Prior to Confession you should carefully examine your conscience.

In the Bible: Acts 3:19; Luke 5:31–32; Jeremiah 31:19
In the Catechism: CCC, 1457, 1458

Going Deeper

God loves healthy relationships and forgiveness is essential to having healthy relationships. Regularly going to God in the Sacrament of Reconciliation and asking for forgiveness is a powerful way to have a fabulous relationship with God. Many of the saints went to Reconciliation every month, some even more often. They knew that going to Confession was the only way to be reconciled to God. They also knew that nothing brought them more joy than having a strong friendship with Jesus.

103. **Q: Does the Sacrament of Reconciliation reconcile us only with God?**

A: No. The Sacrament of Reconciliation reconciles us with God and with the Church.

In the Bible: 1 Corinthians 12:26
In the Catechism: CCC, 1422, 1449, 1469

Going Deeper

God delights in his relationship with you and he delights in your relationship with the Church. Sin makes your soul sick, it hurts other people, and it harms your relationship with God and the Church. When we go to Confession, God forgives us and heals our soul. He also heals our relationship with him and with the Church through the Sacrament of Reconciliation.

104. **Q: How do we experience God's mercy?**

A: We experience God's mercy in the Sacrament of Reconciliation. We also experience God's mercy through the kindness, generosity, and compassion of other people. God's mercy always draws us closer to him. We can also be instruments of God's mercy by exercising the works of mercy with kindness, generosity, and compassion.

In the Bible: Luke 3:11; John 8:11
In the *Catechism*: CCC, 1422, 1449, 2447

Going Deeper

Sometimes when we do something that is wrong we may be tempted to think that God will not love us anymore. But that is never true. God will always love you because our God is a merciful God. God shows us his mercy by forgiving us, teaching us, and caring for our physical and spiritual needs even when we don't deserve it. He shows us his mercy through the Sacrament of Reconciliation and through the loving actions of other people. God invites you to spread his mercy by forgiving others, praying for others, and caring for those in need.

105. **Q: Where in the Church building is Jesus present in a special way?**

A: In the tabernacle.

In the Bible: Exodus 40:34; Luke 22:19
In the *Catechism*: CCC, 1379

106. **Q: Who is the source of all blessings?**

A: God is the source of all blessings. In the Mass we praise and adore God the Father as the source of every blessing in creation. We also thank God the Father for sending us his Son. Most of all we express our gratitude to God the Father for making us his children.

In the Bible: Luke 1:68–79; Psalm 72:18–19
In the *Catechism*: CCC, 1083, 1110

Going Deeper

You are blessed in so many ways. But every blessing comes from the very first blessing—life! God has given you life and made you his child. This is an incredible blessing! One of the greatest ways we can show God our gratitude is by going to Mass. By showing up every Sunday and participating in Mass, you show God how thankful you are for everything he has done for you.

107. **Q: True or False. When you receive Holy Communion, you receive a piece of bread that signifies, symbolizes, or represents Jesus.**

A: False.

In the Bible: Matthew 26:26
In the *Catechism*: CCC, 1374, 1413

108. **Q: What do you receive in Holy Communion?**

A: The Body, Blood, Soul, and Divinity of Christ.

In the Bible: 1 Corinthians 11:24; John 6:54–55
In the *Catechism*: CCC, 1374, 1413

Going Deeper

Jesus is truly present in the Eucharist. It is not a symbol; it is Jesus. We receive all of Jesus in the Eucharist. Even the tiniest crumb that falls from the wafer contains all of Jesus. The bread and wine become Jesus at the moment of Consecration. This is an incredible moment. In this moment Jesus comes among us once again. Every time you go to Mass, bread and wine are transformed into the Body and Blood of Jesus. You are blessed to be able to receive Jesus in the Eucharist.

109. **Q: What is Transubstantiation?**

A: Transubstantiation is when the bread and wine become the Body and Blood of Jesus.

In the Bible: Matthew 26:26; Mark 14:22; Luke 22:19–20
In the *Catechism*: CCC, 1376

Going Deeper

God has the power to transform everyone and everything he comes in contact with. Every day, in every Catholic Church, during every Mass, God transforms ordinary bread and wine into the Body and Blood of Jesus Christ. After receiving Jesus in the Eucharist, many of the saints prayed that they would become what they had received. God answered their prayers and transformed their lives by helping them to live like Jesus. Just like with the saints, God can transform your life. Every time you receive Jesus in the Eucharist worthily, you can become a little more like him. Just like Jesus, you can love generously and serve powerfully everyone you meet.

110. **Q: When does the bread and wine change into the Body and Blood of Christ?**

   A: It is changed by the words and intention of the priest at the moment of Consecration during Mass. The priest, asking for the help of the Holy Spirit, says the same words Jesus said at the Last Supper: "This is my body which will be given up for you . . . This is the cup of my blood . . ."

   In the Bible: Mark 14:22; Luke 22:19–20
   In the *Catechism*: CCC, 1412, 1413

Going Deeper

The Last Supper is the most famous meal in the history of the world. In that room two thousand years ago, Jesus gave himself completely to his Apostles. Every time we come to Mass, the priest recites the same words as Jesus during the Last Supper. When he does, the wheat bread and grape wine become the Body and Blood of Jesus. Amazing! Jesus wants to give himself completely to you just as he gave himself completely to his Apostles at the Last Supper. Jesus wants to be invited into your life. He wants to encourage you, guide you, listen to you, and love you. He offers himself to you in a special way at Mass, especially in the amazing gift of Holy Communion.

111. **Q: What are the benefits of receiving the Body and Blood of Jesus in the Eucharist?**

   A: When you receive Jesus in the Eucharist, you become more united with the Lord, your venial sins are forgiven, and you are given grace to avoid grave sins. Receiving Jesus in the Eucharist also increases your love for

Jesus and reinforces the fact that you are a member of God's family —
the Catholic Church.

In the Bible: John 6:56–57
In the Catechism: CCC, 1391–1396

Going Deeper

The Eucharist empowers us to do great things for God. The saints did
incredible things for God throughout their lives and the Eucharist was the
source of their strength. Through Holy Communion we grow closer to God,
move further away from sinful habits, and grow in love for Jesus and the
Catholic Church. The Eucharist is the ultimate food for your soul, and it
will give you the strength and courage to serve God and others powerfully
just like the saints.

112. **Q: How important is the Eucharist to the life of the Church?**

A: The Eucharist is indispensable in the life of the Church. The Eucharist is the
heart of the Church. One of the reasons the Eucharist is so important to the
life of the Church is because, through it, Jesus unites every member of the
Church with his sacrifice on the cross. Every grace that flows from Jesus'
suffering, death, and Resurrection comes to us through the Church.

In the Bible: John 6:51, 54, 56
In the Catechism: CCC, 1324, 1331, 1368, 1407

Going Deeper

Jesus promised to be with us always, no matter what. He has been keeping this
promise for over 2,000 years. Jesus is always with us in the Eucharist. The
Eucharist unites us to Jesus and his Church. It also unites us to one another.
We are blessed to have the Eucharist. Only through the Catholic Church can
we receive the gift of the Eucharist. We are blessed to be Catholic.

113. **Q: Should you receive Holy Communion in the state of mortal sin?**

A: No. If you do, you commit the additional mortal sin of sacrilege.

In the Bible: 1 Corinthians 11:27–29
In the Catechism: CCC, 1385, 1415, 1457

Going Deeper

If Jesus came to visit your home and it was so messy you couldn't open the door to let Jesus in, that would be terrible. No matter how much Jesus wants to be a part of our lives he will never force himself upon us. Mortal sin slams the door of our souls in Jesus' face. It breaks our relationship with God and prevents the wonderful graces of the Eucharist from flowing into our hearts, minds, and souls. Reconciliation reopens the door to our souls and lets Jesus enter our lives again.

114. **Q: What is sacrilege?**

A: It is the abuse of a sacred person, place, or thing.

> In the Bible: 1 Corinthians 11:27–29
> In the Catechism: CCC, 2120

115. **Q: If you are in a state of mortal sin, what should you do before receiving Holy Communion?**

A: You should go to Confession as soon as possible.

> In the Bible: 2 Corinthians 5:20
> In the Catechism: CCC, 1385, 1457

116. **Q: Who offered the first Mass?**

A: Jesus Christ.

> In the Bible: Mark 14:22–24
> In the Catechism: CCC, 1323

117. **Q: When did Jesus offer the first Mass?**

A: On Holy Thursday night, the night before he died, at the Last Supper.

> In the Bible: Matthew 26:26–28
> In the Catechism: CCC, 1323

118. **Q: Who offers the Eucharistic sacrifice?**

A: Jesus is the eternal high priest. In the Mass, he offers the Eucharistic sacrifice through the ministry of the priest.

In the Bible: Mark 14:22; Matthew 26:26; Luke 22:19; 1 Corinthians 11:24
In the *Catechism*: CCC, 1348

Going Deeper

The Last Supper was the first Eucharistic celebration. This was the Apostles' First Communion, and the first time anybody had ever received the Eucharist. The Mass is not just a symbol of what happened that night. Jesus is truly present in the Eucharist. Every time we receive Holy Communion Jesus gives himself to us in the same way he gave himself to his Apostles over 2,000 years ago. Jesus works through the priest at Mass to transform the bread and wine into his Body and Blood.

119. **Q: What is the Sacrifice of the Mass?**

A: It is the sacrifice of Jesus Christ on Calvary, the memorial of Christ's Passover, made present when the priest repeats the words of Consecration spoken by Jesus over the bread and wine at the Last Supper.

In the Bible: Hebrews 7:25–27
In the *Catechism*: CCC, 1364, 1413

Going Deeper

God loves you so much, and he will go to unimaginable lengths to prove his love for you. On Good Friday Jesus was beaten, bullied, mocked, spat upon, cursed at, and crucified on the cross. Jesus laid down his life for us. On Easter Sunday Jesus rose from the dead. He did this so that we might live a very different life while here on earth and happily with him forever in heaven. Every time we go to Mass we remember the life of Jesus, the path he invites us to walk, and the incredible lengths to which he went to show us his love.

120. **Q: Who can preside at the Eucharist?**

A: Only an ordained priest can preside at the Eucharist and Consecrate the bread and the wine so that they become the Body and Blood of Jesus.

In the Bible: John 13:3–8
In the *Catechism*: CCC, 1411

Going Deeper

To be a priest is a great honor and privilege. Priests lay down their lives to serve God and his people. The priesthood is a life of service. One of the ultimate privileges of the priesthood is standing in Jesus' place and transforming bread and wine into the Eucharist. This privilege is reserved for priests alone. Nobody other than a priest can do this.

121. **Q: How do we participate in the Sacrifice of the Mass?**

A: By uniting ourselves and our intentions to the bread and wine, offered by the priest, which become Jesus' sacrifice to the Father.

In the Bible: Romans 12:1
In the *Catechism*: CCC, 1407

122. **Q: What does the Eucharistic celebration we participate in at Mass always include?**

A: The Eucharist celebration always includes: the proclamation of the Word of God; thanksgiving to God the Father for all his blessings; the Consecration of the bread and wine; and participation in the liturgical banquet by receiving the Lord's Body and Blood. These elements constitute one single act of worship.

In the Bible: Luke 24:13–35
In the *Catechism*: CCC, 1345–1355, 1408

Going Deeper

The Mass follows a certain formula that is always repeated and never changes. You could go to Mass anywhere in the world and you will always find it is the same. At every Mass we read from the Bible, show God our gratitude for the blessing of Jesus, witness bread and wine transformed into the Body and Blood of Jesus, and receive Jesus during Holy Communion. In the midst of this great routine, God wants to surprise you. You could spend a lifetime going to Mass every single day and at the end of your life still be surprised by what God has to say to you in the Mass. The Mass is truly amazing!

123. **Q: What role does music play in the Mass?**

A: Sacred music helps us to worship God.

In the Bible: Psalm 57:8–10; Ephesians 5:19; Hebrews 2:12; Colossians 3:16
In the *Catechism*: CCC, 1156

Going Deeper

Sometimes when we are praying it can be difficult to find the right words
to express how we feel. To help us, God gives us the great gift of sacred
music. Over the course of the Mass there will be songs of praise, songs
of worship, songs of petition, and songs of thanksgiving. Sacred music
helps raise our hearts to God and bond us together as a community
calling out to God with one voice.

124. **Q: What is the Lord's Day?**

A: Sunday is the Lord's Day. It is a day of rest. It is a day to gather as a family. It
is the principal day for celebrating the Eucharist because it is the day of the
Resurrection.

In the Bible: Exodus 31:15; Matthew 28:1; Mark 16:2; John 20:1
In the Catechism: CCC, 1166, 1193, 2174

Going Deeper

Sunday is a very special day. The Resurrection of Jesus is so important that
we celebrate it every day at Mass. But we celebrate the Resurrection of Jesus
in a special way every Sunday. We do that by resting, spending time with
family, and going to Mass. The Lord's Day is a day to marvel at all the amazing
ways God has blessed us, and because of that it is a day of gratitude.

125. **Q: Is it a mortal sin for you to miss Mass on Sunday or a Holy Day through your
own fault?**

A: Yes.

In the Bible: Exodus 20:8
In the Catechism: CCC, 2181

126. **Q: Which person of the Holy Trinity do you receive in Confirmation?**

A: The Holy Spirit.

In the Bible: Romans 8:15
In the Catechism: CCC, 1302

127. **Q: What happens in the Sacrament of Confirmation?**

A: The Holy Spirit comes upon us and strengthens us to be soldiers of Christ, that we may spread and defend the Catholic faith.

In the Bible: John 14:26; 15:26
In the Catechism: CCC, 1303, 2044

128. **Q: What is Confirmation?**

A: Confirmation is a Sacrament that perfects Baptismal grace. Through it we receive the Holy Spirit and are strengthened in grace so we can grow in virtue, live holy lives, and carry out the mission God calls us to.

In the Bible: John 20:22; Acts 2:1—4
In the Catechism: CCC, 1285, 1316

Going Deeper

When you are older you will be blessed to receive the Sacrament of Confirmation. Confirmation reminds us that in Baptism God blessed us with a special mission and filled us with the Holy Spirit. Through an outpouring of the Holy Spirit at Confirmation, we are filled with the courage and wisdom to live out the mission God has given us. Confirmation deepens our friendship with Jesus and the Catholic Church. It reminds us that we are sons and daughters of a great King. It will be a special moment in your life and a wonderful blessing!

129. **Q: When is Confirmation received?**

A: Most Catholics in the West receive Confirmation during their teenage years, but in the East Confirmation is administered immediately after Baptism.

In the Bible: Hebrews 6:1—3
In the Catechism: CCC, 1306, 1318

Going Deeper

Baptism, Confirmation, and First Holy Communion are called the Sacraments of Initiation. In a special way, the Sacraments of Initiation deepen our friendship with Jesus and the Church, fill us with what we need to live out God's mission for our lives, and inspire us to become all that God created us to be. It is important to remember that these three Sacraments are connected. They are the foundation for a fabulous friendship with God on earth and forever in heaven. In some parts of the world, and at different times throughout history, people have received these Sacraments at different times according to local traditions and practical considerations. For example, hundreds of years ago, the bishop may have only visited a village once every two or three years, and so Confirmation would take place when he visited. Even today, some children receive Baptism, First Communion, and Confirmation all at the same time.

130. Q: **What are the Seven Gifts of the Holy Spirit?**
A: Wisdom, understanding, counsel, fortitude, knowledge, piety, and fear of the Lord.

In the Bible: Isaiah 11:2–3
In the *Catechism*: CCC, 1830, 1831

131. Q: **Before you are confirmed, you will promise the bishop that you will never give up the practice of your Catholic faith for anyone or anything. Did you ever make that promise before?**
A: Yes, at Baptism.

In the Bible: Joshua 24:21–22
In the *Catechism*: CCC, 1298

132. Q: **Most of you were baptized as little babies. How could you make that promise?**
A: Our parents and godparents made that promise for us.

In the Bible: Mark 16:16
In the *Catechism*: CCC, 1253

133. Q: **What kind of sin is it to receive Confirmation in the state of mortal sin?**
A: A sacrilege.

In the Bible: 1 Corinthians 11:27–29
In the *Catechism*: CCC, 2120

134. **Q: If you have committed mortal sin, what should you do before receiving Confirmation?**

A: You should make a good Confession.

In the Bible: 2 Corinthians 5:20; Luke 15:18
In the Catechism: CCC, 1310

135. **Q: What are the three traditional vocations?**

A: Married life, Holy Orders, and the consecrated life.

In the Bible: Ephesians 5:31–32; Hebrews 5:6, 7:11; Psalm 110:4; Matthew 19:12; 1 Corinthians 7:34–66
In the Catechism: CCC, 914, 1536, 1601

136. **Q: What are the three vows that a consecrated man or woman takes?**

A: Chastity, Poverty, and Obedience.

In the Bible: Matthew 19:21; Matthew 19:12; 1 Corinthians 7:34–36; Hebrews 10:7
In the Catechism: CCC, 915

137. **Q: What are the three ranks (degrees) of Holy Orders?**

A: Deacon, Priest, and Bishop.

In the Bible: 1 Timothy 4:14; 2 Timothy 1:6–7
In the Catechism: CCC, 1554

138. **Q: For whom did God make marriage?**

A: One man and one woman.

In the Bible: Genesis 1:26–28; Ephesians 5:31
In the Catechism: CCC, 1601, 2360

139. **Q: Is it possible for two men or two women to get married?**

A: No.

In the Bible: Genesis 19:1–29; Romans 1:24–27; 1 Corinthians 6:9
In the Catechism: CCC, 2357, 2360

140. **Q: When can a man and woman begin living together?**

A: Only after their marriage.

> In the Bible: 1 Corinthians 6:18–20
> In the Catechism: CCC, 235

141. **Q: What are the three marriage promises a husband and wife make to each other?**

A: Faithfulness, permanence, and being open to having children.

> In the Bible: Matthew 19:6; Genesis 1:28
> In the Catechism: CCC, 1640, 1641, 1664

142. **Q: Why is abortion wrong?**

A: Because it takes the life of a baby in its mother's womb.

> In the Bible: Jeremiah 1:5; Psalm 139:13
> In the Catechism: CCC, 2270

143. **Q: How many commandments are there?**

A: Ten.

> In the Bible: Exodus 20:1–18; Deuteronomy 5:6–21
> In the Catechism: CCC, 2054

144. **Q: What are the Ten Commandments?**

A:
1. I, the Lord, am your God. You shall not have other gods besides me.
2. You shall not take the name of the Lord, your God, in vain.
3. Remember to keep holy the Lord's Day.
4. Honor your father and mother.
5. You shall not kill.
6. You shall not commit adultery.
7. You shall not steal.
8. You shall not bear false witness against your neighbor.
9. You shall not covet your neighbor's wife.
10. You shall not covet your neighbor's goods.

> In the Bible: Exodus 20:1–18; Deuteronomy 5:6–21
> In the Catechism: CCC, 496, 497

145. Q: What are the four main kinds of prayer?

A: The four main kinds of prayer are adoration, thanksgiving, petition, and intercession.

In the Bible: Psalm 95:6; Colossians 4:2; James 5:16; 1 John 3:22
In the Catechism: CCC, 2628, 2629, 2634, 2638, 2639

146. Q: How often should we pray?

A: Every day.

In the Bible: 1 Thessalonians 5:17; Luke 18:1
In the Catechism: CCC, 2742

Acknowledgments

This project began with a dream: to create the best First Reconciliation and First Communion experience in the world. For the millions of young souls that will experience this program we hope we have delivered on that dream.

Hundreds of people have poured their time, talent, and expertise into *Blessed*. It is the result of years of research, development, and testing. To everyone who has contributed—and you know who you are—in every stage of the process: Thank You! May God bless you and reward you richly for your generosity.

Special thanks to: Jack Beers, Bridget Eichold, Katie Ferrara, Allen and Anita Hunt, Steve Lawson, Mark Moore, Shawna Navaro, Father Robert Sherry, and Ben Skudlarek.

Beyond the enormous talent contributions, others have been incredibly generous with their money. *Blessed* was funded by a group of incredibly generous donors. It will now be made available at no cost to every parish in North America. This is one of the many ways that this program is unique.

Everything great in history has been accomplished by people who believed that the future could be better than the past. Thank you for believing!

Now we offer *Blessed* to the Church as a gift, hopeful that it will help young Catholics encounter Jesus and discover the genius of Catholicism.

Blessed was:

Written by: Matthew Kelly
Illustrated by: Carolina Farias
Designed by: The Dynamic Catholic Design Team
Principal designers: Ben Hawkins and Jenny Miller

Help *Blessed* become The-Best-Version-of-Itself

Blessed is different from other programs in a hundred ways. One way that it is different is that it is always changing and improving. We need your help with this. Whether you find a typo or think of some fun way to improve the program, please email us and tell us about it so that year after year Blessed can become even more dynamic.

blessed@dynamiccatholic.com

Blessed

The Dynamic Catholic First Reconciliation Experience
©2017 The Dynamic Catholic Institute and Kakadu, LLC.

The Scripture quotations contained herein are from *The Catholic Edition of the Revised Standard Version Bible*, copyright © 1965, 1966 by the Division of Christian Education of the National Council of the Churches of Christ in the U.S.A., and are used by permission.

This volume contains quotes and excerpts from a number of titles previously released by Matthew Kelly. The copyright to these works are held by Kakadu, LLC. These quotes and excerpts have been made available to Dynamic Catholic for use in this volume, but the copyright to these quotes and excerpts remains the property of Kakadu, LLC.

Dynamic Catholic®. Be Bold. Be Catholic.® and The-Best-Version-of-Yourself® are registered trademarks of the Dynamic Catholic Institute.

ISBN 978-1-63582-018-8

FIRST EDITION
Seventh printing, February 2022